M000303134

The

·GILBERT· ·SCOTT·

Also by Marcus Wareing
and published by Bantam Press

NUTMEG AND CUSTARD

The · GILBERT · SCOTT ·
BOOK OF BRITISH FOOD

Marcus Wareing with Chantelle Nicholson

BANTAM PRESS

LONDON · TORONTO · SYDNEY · AUCKLAND · JOHANNESBURG

TRANSWORLD PUBLISHERS
61–63 Uxbridge Road, London W5 5SA
A Random House Group Company
www.transworldbooks.co.uk

First published in Great Britain
in 2013 by Bantam Press
an imprint of Transworld Publishers

A CIP catalogue record for this book
is available from the British Library.

ISBN 9780593070437

Addresses for Random House Group Ltd companies outside the UK
can be found at: www.randomhouse.co.uk
The Random House Group Ltd Reg. No. 954009

Photography: Sergio Coimbra

Design: White Label Productions Ltd. ᴡᴘ⦂

Typeset in Garamond and Perpetua

Printed and bound in Italy by Graphicom

2 4 6 8 10 9 7 5 3 1

The Gilbert Scott opened its doors to the public on the 5th May 2011, exactly 138 years to the day after the official opening of the Midland Grand hotel.

·INTRODUCTION·

How it all began

In 1865 the Midland Railway company held a competition for the design of a hotel, with the brief that it needed to 'add lustre' to their soon-to-be-completed St Pancras station. A number of architects submitted their schemes, with George Gilbert Scott's wondrous 300-bedroom design being declared the winner. (A leading Gothic Revivalist, Scott restored and designed many iconic buildings all over the Empire, including the Albert Memorial in London.) Construction of the Midland Grand hotel began in 1868 and it opened officially on 5th May 1873 – 138 years to the day before the opening of The Gilbert Scott restaurant.

The hotel oozed extravagance. The Victorian decor was luxurious, with extensive decoration in gold leaf and open fires in every room. Ornate stencilling and flamboyant wallpapers embellished every inch of the hotel. In the 'Coffee Room' (which is now The Gilbert Scott restaurant), pillars of polished limestone lined the walls, their gilded capitals carved with conkers, pea pods and bursting pomegranates.

For a building of this size and style, which required the use of gas lighting, every trick was used in the construction to allow as much natural light in as possible: huge rooms with huge windows; ornate, Gothic fanlights above every door; and wonderfully arched stairwells. The most famous of these, widely considered the most majestic in the country, is the Grand Staircase, which is a fantastic example of high-Victorian Gothic decoration. Altogether, the total cost of the building added up to £438,000 (approximately £438m today).

The Midland Grand's reputation was quickly cemented and it was widely recognized as one of London's leading hotels, the most expensive apart from The Langham on Portland Place. Guests of note during the hotel's heyday included Jesse Boot (of Boots the chemist), the actress

Marie Lloyd, 'Commodore' Cornelius Vanderbilt, one of America's richest men, and the American inventor and industrialist George Pullman.

Innovations didn't stop upon the hotel opening: in 1899 a specially designed revolving door was fitted in the hall entrance, and in the same year electric lifts were installed, replacing the original water-driven ones.

After a wondrous 62 years of welcoming guests, the hotel became too expensive to maintain and heat. Another factor contributing to its decline was that its handsome rooms came without bathrooms. When the hotel was built the fact that there were bathrooms at all (five in total, with nine baths for the 300 rooms) was a novelty.

Unfortunately, as en-suite bathrooms became more and more commonplace, it was impossible to introduce the necessary plumbing in order to bring the Midland up to the standards of its competitors. Despite novelties such as a Moroccan coffee house and an in-house orchestra, the hotel couldn't be saved, and it closed its doors in 1935.

During the Second World War the building was bombed three times in one month but as credit to the strength of its construction it emerged almost completely unscathed. In 1948 it became the headquarters for British Transport Hotels and remained so until a failed fire certificate forced them out in 1985.

What at its opening was called 'the most perfect in every possible respect in the world' came to be known as a 'gigantic haunted house', outdated and obsolete. There were attempts to demolish the building, until a Grade I listing in 1967 ensured its survival. In 1993–5, £9 million of public money was spent on restoring the exterior. But the building itself remained unused.

When it was under threat of demolition, Sir John Betjeman said that the Midland Grand hotel was 'too beautiful and too romantic to survive'. He was mistaken: it has survived for precisely these reasons and has now been lovingly restored to its former grandeur, once again welcoming hotel guests, now as the St Pancras Hotel.

The Gilbert Scott

The Gilbert Scott came about due to one man's vision – that of Harry Handelsman. Harry saw deeper than the dilapidated, run-down and tired monstrosity in a not-so-great part of town. Due to his vision, I – along with my team – am lucky enough to operate a restaurant and bar in what I consider is London's most beautiful building.

The incarnation of The Gilbert Scott began in November 2009 when I received an email from a commercial lettings agent inviting me to look at a restaurant site in St Pancras. Given Mayfair had been my stomping ground since I began my restaurant career, I was a little hesitant to go so far north. But I thought it was worth a look. My wife Jane, my then Senior Sous Chef/Operations Manager, Chantelle Nicholson, and I went to check it out. We were given a tour of the building by a fascinating man named Royden Stock. What he did not know about the building or its architect, Sir George Gilbert Scott, is not worth knowing.

After the show-round we went next door to the British Library for a coffee. I asked Jane and Chantelle what their thoughts were. There was a little moment of silence and then we all grinned and agreed in unison that it was the perfect site for our next venture. We met Harry a few weeks later to make our pitch – explaining why we wanted the site and what we thought we could do with it. Thankfully, Harry liked our vision and granted us the site.

Now began the mammoth task of turning our vision and our ideas into reality. With Chantelle at the helm as General Manager, spearheading the project, we went through the brainstorm of creating what was to become The Gilbert Scott. We really wanted to bring to life the history of the building and to give due respect to the incredible man who designed it, naming our restaurant The Gilbert Scott in his honour. We had a firm conviction to be a British restaurant, with the dishes on our menu giving a nod to our country's culinary history.

Chantelle, who by then had spent six years in my kitchens, worked on all aspects of the new restaurant, including the first menu. Research revealed many fascinating things about historical British food as well as about the wondrous building and the new King's Cross/St Pancras community we were about to join.

One of our recipe sources was, of course, the cookery book by the esteemed Mrs Beeton. While a lot of the recipes in her *Book of Household Management* call for now-unused measurements (a 'gill' – a quarter of a pint) and a lot of suet and lard – as well as lobster and truffles, which weren't thought out of the ordinary for your average home cook – there were the bones of some great dishes there for us to build on. Another source was John Nott, cook to the Duke of Bolton, whose 1723 book is noted as 'The Choicest Receipts in all the several Branches of Cookery; or the best and newest Ways of dressing all sorts of Flesh, Fish, Fowl, &c. for a Common or Noble Table; with their proper Garniture and Sauces'. Nott discusses how to create the most magical banquets with live birds stuffed inside cooked animals, which fly out when the meat is carved.

This book gives a small insight into the functioning of a working restaurant and bar, as well as taking a journey through some of our country's historical cuisine. Let's face it, British food hasn't enjoyed a fantastic reputation, both here at home and in the wider world, but I do believe this is slowly changing, influenced by the fabulous produce we can offer, as well as the great restaurants already established here and adventurous home cooks. I do hope you enjoy reading and trying the recipes in this book.

BAR

Our bar at The Gilbert Scott is probably my favourite space in the entire building. It was the original entrance lobby to the Hotel and has a grand revolving door to bring guests through. The ceiling is two storeys high and has the most amazing intricate pattern painted on it.

The bar is open all day, from early morning to the very early morning! We serve breakfast, snacks and afternoon tea as well as some pretty amazing cocktails. I had never run a bar before this, and I now see how the bartender's job is similar to that of a chef. Both create a very special product from raw ingredients using their knowledge, skill and technique. Cocktails really are a work of art and can be even more intricate than a dish on the menu. Flavour, texture and appearance are just as important with any cocktail as they are in cooking. Ensuring you have good-quality ingredients to work with is the starting point for both too.

In the future, we hope to have a terrace out the front – a sort of gin garden area – so fingers crossed it comes together for you to enjoy.

·COCKTAILS·

Each of the following cocktails will serve 2.

1

· GEORGE'S FIZZ ·

Named in honour of Sir George Gilbert Scott, this is a light and refreshing cocktail. The potato vodka, made by Chase in England, gives it a creamy texture and the Kümmel, infused with caraway, cumin and fennel, adds another dimension.

6 slices lemon
80ml Chase potato vodka
pinch of saffron threads
20ml peach schnapps
10ml Kümmel
30ml sugar syrup (see page 25)
ice cubes
soda water

Muddle the lemon slices with the vodka and saffron in a cocktail shaker or a Boston glass. Alternatively, use the end of a rolling pin in a larger container to gently pound the ingredients together. Add all remaining ingredients, except the soda water, and shake with ice. Strain into two flutes and top up with soda water.

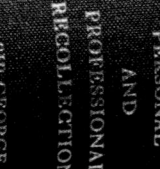

2

· RUM AND GINGER AWAKENING ·

This is one of our brunch cocktails and it does just what it says – awakens you! It is fresh, clean and easy drinking. Sample a few spiced rums until you find your favourite.

80ml spiced dark rum
20g fresh root ginger, peeled and freshly grated
50ml apple juice
30ml fresh lime juice
crushed ice
100ml ginger beer

Shake together all the ingredients, except the ginger beer. Strain into two tall glasses over crushed ice and top up with the ginger beer.

· A-PEAR-ITIF ·

This fantastic cocktail was created by the talented Dav Eames, our current bar manager. It combines cucumber, elderflower and pear vodka to create a really refreshing drink that looks stunning.

50g cucumber, chopped
50ml Grey Goose La Poire vodka
50ml Bombay Sapphire gin
50ml elderflower cordial
50ml fresh lime juice
ice cubes

To garnish
2 long, thin strips cucumber
2 ice cubes

Muddle the cucumber with the vodka in a cocktail shaker. Alternatively, use the end of a rolling pin in a larger container to gently pound the cucumber and vodka together. Add the remaining ingredients, shake well and strain into two coupette glasses. Garnish each with a cucumber-wrapped ice cube.

· GOOD FOR THE GOOSE ·

One of the first cocktails we put on our list, this was created by our first bar manager, Oliver Blackburn, paying tribute to the very fine range of vodkas from Grey Goose. Combining orange vodka, honey and marmalade, topped up with English sparkling wine, it really is an elegant tipple.

50ml Grey Goose L'Orange vodka
40ml fresh lemon juice
1 tbsp marmalade
1 tbsp honey
4 dashes of orange bitters
ice cubes
80ml Ridgeview Blanc de Noirs
(English sparkling wine)

Put all the ingredients, except the sparkling wine, into a cocktail shaker or jar, cover and shake. Strain into two flutes, dividing evenly, then top up with the sparkling wine.

5

· ST PANCRAS SUNRISE ·

Paying homage to the revitalized King's Cross/ St Pancras area, this cocktail uses the wonderfully fragrant Hendrick's gin. One of the botanicals used in this gin is cucumber, which makes it delightfully fresh. This is a colourful cocktail, great for a summer's evening.

80ml Hendrick's gin
20ml Cazadores Blanco tequila
40ml pomegranate juice
ice cubes
40ml fresh orange juice
80ml bitter lemon
2 twists of orange peel, to garnish

Shake the gin, tequila and pomegranate juice together with ice. Strain into two cut-crystal wine glasses. Slowly add the orange juice followed by the bitter lemon. Garnish each glass with an orange twist.

6

· QUEEN MOTHER'S COCKTAIL ·

The late Queen Mother was rumoured to have enjoyed Dubonnet, a blend of fortified wine, herbs and spices, and this cocktail (pictured right), created by Oli Blackburn, is named for her. It also includes a great English sparkling wine, Nyetimber, which is produced in East Sussex.

20ml Chase marmalade vodka
20ml Chase potato vodka
40ml Dubonnet
50ml fresh lemon juice
10ml Benedictine
dash of orange bitters
ice cubes
80ml Nyetimber Classic Cuvée
(English sparkling wine)

Shake all the ingredients, except the sparkling wine, with ice. Strain into two Champagne saucers and top up with the sparkling wine.

7

· THE EARL OF GREY ·

We have sometimes served this tea-based cocktail with our afternoon tea offering. The bergamot in Earl Grey tea works very well with the richness of the Cognac, creating an elegant drink that is great as an after-dinner tipple too.

60ml Cognac
5g Earl Grey tea leaves
10ml crème d'abricots (apricot liqueur)
10ml Amaretto Disarronno (almond liqueur)
dash of apricot bitters
grated zest of ½ fresh bergamot orange
crushed ice
80ml ginger ale

Warm the Cognac slightly, then add the tea. Cover and leave to infuse for 2 hours. Strain through a fine sieve. Shake the Cognac with the other ingredients, except the ice and ginger ale, then strain into two rocks glasses over crushed ice. Top up with the ginger ale.

To The Gilbert Scott team, past, present and future. To your creativity, passion, commitment, hard work and great personalities (and wonderful cocktails!).

CONTENTS

10

· COUNTESS MORPHY'S · CROQUETTES

A 'Countess Morphy' wrote a book entitled *Recipes of All Nations* in the 1930s, which contained a fascinating collection of recipes from all around the world. These little croquettes make a good snack with drinks.

Serves 4

40g butter
½ onion, peeled and finely diced
25ml milk
225g plain mashed potatoes,
at room temperature
50g self-raising flour
salt
vegetable oil, for deep-frying
lemon mayonnaise or Tendring Hall
Ketchup (see page 33), to serve

To coat
plain flour
2 free-range eggs, beaten
about 75g panko breadcrumbs

Heat 15g of the butter in a small pan and cook the onion until softened. Remove from the heat.

Beat the remaining butter and the milk into the mashed potatoes, then mix in the onion and self-raising flour. Season with a little salt. Roll into cylinders about 8cm long and 3cm in diameter. Dust with plain flour, then coat in beaten egg followed by panko crumbs. As the cylinders are coated, transfer to a tray. Cover and place in the fridge to chill and set for at least 25 minutes.

Heat oil for deep-frying to 175°C. Fry the croquettes, in batches, until golden brown all over and heated through (test by inserting the tip of a knife into the centre of a croquette, then touch the knife to check that it is hot). Serve the croquettes straightaway, with lemon mayonnaise or Tendring Hall ketchup.

11

· SALT AND PEPPER SQUID ·

Although not strictly a British dish by origin, this does make
a great bar snack. The squid is not cooked in a batter, but is just
dusted with aromatic pepper and a good dose of salt.

Serves 4

300g squid, cleaned
1 tsp Maldon sea salt
½ tsp black peppercorns
½ tsp Sichuan peppercorns
1 tbsp cornflour
oil for deep-frying

To prepare the squid, remove the tentacles and slice them
into small bunches. Halve each squid body, then score in
a criss-cross pattern using a sharp knife. Cut the squid bodies
into pieces about 5cm square and set aside on kitchen paper.

Lightly pulse the salt and peppercorns together in a spice
mill or coffee grinder until very fine. Mix with the cornflour
in a shallow dish.

Heat oil for deep-frying to 170°C. When up to temperature,
lightly coat the squid with the seasoned mix, then fry briefly,
in batches, for no more than 30–45 seconds, until golden
brown. Drain on kitchen paper and keep hot. Serve as soon
as all the squid has been cooked.

SOUTHWOLD FRIED WHITEBAIT
WITH TENDRING HALL KETCHUP

Very easy to prepare, this is a wonderfully tasty bar snack. The crisp whitebait go so well with a tangy home-made tomato ketchup.

Serves 4

Tendring Hall ketchup
600g ripe tomatoes, halved lengthways
1 tsp salt
freshly ground black pepper to taste
1 small onion, peeled and sliced
2 cloves garlic, peeled and crushed
50ml olive oil
1 red chilli, deseeded and finely chopped
1 tbsp soft brown sugar
100ml white wine vinegar

Whitebait
5 tbsp plain flour
½ tsp cayenne pepper
1 tsp smoked paprika
½ tsp salt
100ml milk
oil for deep-frying
250g whitebait (fresh or thawed frozen)

Preheat the oven to 200°C/400°F/gas mark 6. To make the ketchup, lay the tomato halves, cut side up, on a roasting tray. Season with the salt and pepper to taste, then scatter the onion and garlic over the tomatoes. Drizzle over the olive oil. Place in the oven and roast for about 30 minutes, until the tomatoes start to break down to a pulp.

Put the chilli, sugar and vinegar in a large saucepan and bring to the boil. Boil for 5 minutes. Scrape the tomato mixture into the pan and stir to mix. Simmer for about 5 minutes, stirring occasionally. Push through a fine sieve into a clean saucepan. Bring to a simmer again and cook for 20 minutes, stirring from time to time. Check the seasoning and adjust if necessary, then allow to cool. Store the ketchup, covered, in the fridge.

For the whitebait, mix together the flour, cayenne pepper, paprika, salt and some black pepper in a mixing bowl or plastic bag. Put the milk in another bowl, and have a sieve placed over a clean mixing bowl alongside. Heat oil for deep-frying to 170°C.

When the oil is up to temperature, put the whitebait into the seasoned flour and toss well to ensure all the fish are coated. Lift them into the sieve and shake over the clean bowl so the excess flour goes into it. Tip the fish into the milk and gently coat, then drain in the sieve, discarding the milk. Place back in the flour mix in the clean bowl, shaking and tossing to coat. Drop the fish into the hot oil, a few at a time to ensure they do not stick together, and fry for 2–3 minutes, until golden all over and crisp. Drain on kitchen paper to remove excess oil, then serve immediately with the ketchup.

· SMOKED MACKEREL PÂTÉ ·

We source our mackerel from a supplier on the Cornish coast and it is delicious. This pâté keeps for a few days in the fridge, so you can use it in a number of ways – as a spread with crusty bread, in a toasted sandwich with a slice of melted Gruyère, or dolloped on a salad.

Serves 4

25g crème fraîche
50g cream cheese
25g home-made or good-quality purchased mayonnaise
grated zest and juice of ½ lemon
10 drops Tabasco sauce
½ tsp salt
freshly ground black pepper to taste
250g smoked mackerel fillet, skinned and flaked

Mix together the crème fraîche, cheese and mayonnaise until smooth. Add the lemon zest and juice, Tabasco, salt and a few good turns of pepper. Add the mackerel and fold through the mix. Check the seasoning and adjust if necessary before serving.

· MUSHROOM PASTIES ·

Cornish pasties, filled with beef, potato, turnip and onions, are deservedly popular. We created this vegetarian version with a rich mushroom filling to serve in our bar – perfect with a cocktail or two.

Makes 4

Pastry
340g plain flour
½ tsp salt
150g cold unsalted butter, diced
1 free-range egg, beaten
a little milk
beaten free-range egg yolk, for glazing

Mushroom filling
2 tbsp vegetable oil
150g button mushrooms, quartered
150g field mushrooms, diced into 1cm pieces
1 tbsp red wine vinegar
25g butter
4 tbsp double cream
leaves from ¼ bunch of thyme
2 tbsp crème fraîche

For the pastry, put the flour and salt in a bowl and rub in the butter until the mix resembles breadcrumbs. Add the egg and enough milk to bind to a stiff dough, being careful not to over-mix. Shape into a ball, wrap in clingfilm and place in the fridge to chill for 20 minutes.

Meanwhile, make the mushroom filling. Heat 1 tablespoon of the oil in a pan, add the button mushrooms with a good pinch of salt and cook until golden and all of the liquid has evaporated. Tip the mushrooms into a colander and set aside. Repeat with the field mushrooms, using the remaining oil.

Add the vinegar to the pan and heat until it is bubbling, then about 1 minute later add the butter. Return all the mushrooms to the pan. Add the double cream and thyme, stirring to mix, and cook for 1 minute. Transfer half of the mushrooms to a blender or food processor and blend to a purée. Return this purée to the remaining mushrooms in the pan and add the crème fraîche with seasoning to taste. Transfer the mushroom mix to a shallow dish and cool, then cover with clingfilm and place in the fridge to firm.

Remove the pastry dough from the fridge and divide into six equal portions. Roll out each portion on a floured work surface and cut out a 15cm diameter round.

Divide the mushroom mix among the six pastry rounds, spooning it on to one half and leaving a 2cm edge clear. Brush the pastry edge with egg yolk, then fold over the empty half to make a half moon shape and press the edges to seal well. Crimp together with your fingers. Chill for 20 minutes.

Preheat the oven to 180°C/350°F/gas mark 4. Place the pasties on a baking tray lined with baking parchment and brush liberally with egg yolk. Bake for 15–20 minutes, until lightly golden. Serve hot.

· TO BEGIN ·

The dishes in this chapter are very versatile, in that they can be served as a starter in a multi-course menu or simply enjoyed for lunch with bread, salad or another accompaniment. In common with all of our cooking at the restaurant, the recipes are inspired by traditional British cuisine and have been created to showcase British produce in season.

I feel strongly about the importance of cooking with – and eating – what is best at a particular time of year. One of my favourite early summer starters here is asparagus with burnt butter hollandaise, and my pick of the dishes during the winter months is Dorset snails with bone marrow. Both of these make the most of seasonal ingredients and seem just right for the expected – or hoped for – weather.

· PRAWN COCKTAIL ·

The prawn cocktail was 'the' starter to serve at any good
dinner party in the UK between 1950 and 1970. It is still
a great combination of flavours and textures, especially with
the abundance of quality shellfish in this country.

Serves 4

*250g good-quality, freshly cooked and
peeled prawns (leave the heads on
4 prawns if you wish, to garnish)
3 medium-sized baby gem lettuces
½ bulb fennel, feathery fronds
reserved to garnish
1 tsp Chardonnay vinegar
2 tbsp olive oil
25g butter
4 slices soft brown bread, crusts
removed, roughly diced*

Cocktail sauce

*100g home-made or good-quality
purchased mayonnaise
2 tbsp tomato ketchup
1 tsp Worcestershire sauce
a few good drops of Tabasco sauce
½ tsp grated lemon zest*

Mix together all of the ingredients for the cocktail sauce.
Put the prawns in a mixing bowl and add enough cocktail
sauce to coat them. Set aside.

Remove most of the outer leaves from the lettuces and
shred them. Place in a bowl. Slice the remaining core
of each lettuce lengthways in half and peel off the leaves.
Finely slice the fennel (use a mandolin if you have one) and
add to the shredded lettuce. Mix together the wine vinegar
and olive oil. Use to dress the lettuce and fennel, and the
halved lettuce leaves. Season well.

Melt the butter in a small saucepan and cook until it begins
to caramelize and turn golden. Remove from the heat. Add
a pinch of salt and then the diced bread, and toss to coat
well with the butter.

Build the salads in four glass bowls or glasses by making
a layer of shredded lettuce and fennel, lettuce heart leaves
and brown bread dice, finishing with the prawns. Dress
with the remaining cocktail sauce and sprinkle with the
chopped fennel fronds. Serve immediately.

16

· PORK PIE ·

Everyone loves a good pork pie and although it takes time to make one yourself, the effort is worth it. Served with a good spoonful of piquant piccalilli, it's a winner for a weekend lunch at any time of year.

Makes 1 large pie or 4 small pies

200g boneless pork belly, half diced
into 5mm cubes, half minced
100g smoked bacon, diced into 5mm cubes
300g boneless pork shoulder, minced
1 tsp ground mace
2 tbsp finely chopped sage
2 tsp finely chopped thyme leaves
a little oil for frying
6 leaves gelatine
300ml chicken stock

Hot water crust pastry
150g lard
220ml water
450g plain flour
½ tsp salt
1 free-range egg yolk, lightly beaten

Mix all the meats with the mace, herbs and some salt and pepper in a bowl. Fry a little of the mix to check the seasoning; adjust if necessary. Cover the bowl and set aside.

Next, make the pastry. Put the lard and water in a large saucepan and bring to the boil (beware of it spitting once hot). Mix the flour and salt together in a bowl. Pour in the hot water and lard mix and stir well, then bring together with your hands.

Roll out the pastry on a floured board and cut the case and the lid for your pie dish(es) – use a 23cm springform cake tin for a large pie or four 11cm springform tins for small pies. Grease the tin, then line carefully with the pastry for the case. Place the lined tin, as well as the pastry lid, on a tray lined with baking parchment and leave in the fridge for 20 minutes to rest and firm up.

Preheat the oven to 180°C/350°F/gas mark 4. Pack the pork mix into the pastry case, then cover with the pastry lid, sealing the join well with egg yolk wash. Make a hole in the centre of the lid to allow the steam to escape during baking and so you can pour in the jelly after cooking. Brush the lid with egg wash, then set the pie on a baking tray and bake for 1½ hours, or 1 hour for small pies, until the pastry is golden brown. Allow to cool.

Soak the gelatine leaves in cold water for 10 minutes, until soft, then squeeze out the water. Heat 100ml of the stock. Season, then add the gelatine and stir until melted. Add the remaining stock and stir. Pour slowly into the pie through the hole in the lid. Place in the fridge to set for at least 3 hours. Serve at room temperature.

· BAKED ONIONS ·

These onions are a great vegetarian starter, satisfyingly packed with almonds.
They also make a delicious accompaniment for a roast joint of meat.

Serves 4

*4 large onions (or 8 small onions), peeled
but with the root left intact
50g butter*

Stuffing
*50g butter
2 shallots, peeled and finely diced
2 cloves garlic, peeled and finely crushed
50g toasted flaked almonds
1 tbsp chopped sage
1 tbsp chopped parsley
1 tsp picked thyme leaves
½ tsp freshly grated nutmeg,
plus extra for serving
4 slices white bread, crusts removed,
made into crumbs*

Begin by cooking the onions. Preheat your oven to 180°C/350°F/gas mark 4. Heat the butter in an ovenproof frying pan and, when foaming, add the onions. Cook until they are nicely browned all over, basting with the butter and turning them so they colour evenly. Transfer to the oven to finish cooking for 10–15 minutes, until they are soft.

Remove from the oven (leave the oven on) and allow to cool slightly, then cut off about a third from the top and gently pull out the root and the centre from each onion, leaving two or three layers intact. Set the onion shells and lids aside. Dice the onion centres you've removed.

For the stuffing, melt the butter in a frying pan over a moderate heat. Add the shallots and garlic, season and cook until soft. Add the diced baked onion together with the toasted almonds, herbs and nutmeg, mixing well, then slowly stir in the breadcrumbs to make a firm consistency. Spoon this stuffing into the onion shells and replace the lids. Set the onions in a baking dish.

Reheat in the oven for about 10 minutes. Finish by grating a little more nutmeg over the top, then serve hot.

· CHILLED BROAD BEAN, ·
PEA AND BLACK OLIVE SOUP

This is a fresh, summery soup, enhanced by the saltiness of black olives paired with the sweetness of peas. Serve it on a summer's day with a chilled bottle of English sparkling wine like the Nyetimber Blanc de Blancs.

Serves 4

2 tbsp vegetable oil
1 small onion, peeled and finely sliced
100g green of leek, finely sliced
500ml vegetable stock
250g frozen peas, thawed
100g cooked, skinned broad beans
(fresh or thawed frozen)
100g spinach
1 tbsp Chardonnay or white wine vinegar
squeeze of lime juice
80g pitted Kalamata olives
100ml olive oil
pea shoots, to garnish (optional)

Heat the vegetable oil in a large saucepan. Add the onion and leek and cook until soft, without browning. Pour in the vegetable stock, season and bring to the boil. Add the peas and broad beans and cook for 2 minutes. Add the spinach and cook for a further 1 minute, then remove from the heat.

Purée the soup in a blender, leaving it a little chunky if you prefer. Chill it as quickly as possible, preferably in a metal container set over ice, stirring continuously, so the soup retains its vibrant green colour.

Add the vinegar and lime juice. Taste and add more seasoning if needed. If the soup is too thick, add a little more cold vegetable stock.

Purée the olives to a paste, then mix with the olive oil. Serve the soup topped with a good drizzle of the oil and a few pea shoots if available.

19

ENGLISH ASPARAGUS
WITH BURNT BUTTER HOLLANDAISE

The English asparagus season is one of my favourite, albeit sadly brief, food
times. To prepare the juicy spears, you only need to snap the woody ends
off, then cook in salted water. The burnt butter hollandaise has a wonderful
nuttiness, and with the asparagus creates one of summer's blissful combinations.

Start by making the reduction for the sauce. Combine the
shallot, garlic, bay leaf, coriander, peppercorns and vinegar in
a small pan and bring to the boil. Simmer rapidly until you
have reduced the mix by just over half. Strain through a fine
sieve into a bowl and set the liquid aside; discard the
ingredients in the sieve.

Next, prepare the burnt butter. Dice the butter into chunks
and place in a saucepan over a moderate heat. When the
butter begins to foam, start whisking it slowly. Cook,
whisking, until it turns a deep golden colour. Remove from
the heat and carefully pour into a heatproof jug. Set aside.

Put the egg yolks in a heatproof bowl, set over a pan of gently
simmering water and whisk until soft and fluffy. Slowly
drizzle the warm burnt butter into the yolks, whisking well.
When the mix has thickened, add a little of the reduction to
taste, then season. Remove the bowl of hollandaise from the
pan of water, cover with clingfilm and keep warm.

Bring a large pan of salted water to the boil. Add the
asparagus and cook until just tender. Drain well, then
serve with lashings of hollandaise.

Serves 4

500g English asparagus, trimmed

Hollandaise sauce
1 small shallot, peeled and sliced
1 clove garlic, peeled and sliced
1 bay leaf
3 coriander seeds
2 white peppercorns
100ml white wine vinegar
125g unsalted butter
3 free-range egg yolks

20

DORSET CRAB, PICKLED PEAR, LEMON CONFIT AND FENNEL

A great dish for any time of year, this is fresh and vibrant – like a visit to the seaside. There are two different parts of the common brown crab that can be eaten: the white meat and the softer brown meat. This recipe incorporates both.

Serves 4

Pickled pears
100g caster sugar
100ml water
50ml white wine vinegar
juice of 1 lemon
1 cinnamon stick
3 cloves
2 star anise
2 ripe but firm pears

Lemon confit
150ml water
75g caster sugar
1 lemon, finely sliced

Crab
50g brown crab meat
2 tbsp good-quality mayonnaise
1 tsp lemon juice
300g picked white crab meat

To serve
1 bulb fennel
50g frisée
baby cress

Begin by pickling the pears. (These are also really good with cheese, so make double the quantity if you have the time.) Put the sugar, water, vinegar, lemon juice and spices in a pan and bring to the boil, then reduce to a simmer. Peel and quarter the pears; remove the cores. Place in the simmering syrup and cover with a disc of greaseproof paper or baking parchment to keep the pears immersed. Simmer gently until tender. Remove from the heat. Using a slotted spoon, lift the pears into a bowl. Cool them and the syrup separately, then store the pears in the syrup in a covered container (they can be kept in the fridge for up to 5 days).

For the lemon confit, bring the water and sugar to the boil in a small pan, stirring to dissolve the sugar, then reduce to a simmer. Add the lemon slices and cover with a disc of greaseproof paper or baking parchment to keep the lemon slices immersed. Simmer very gently for 25 minutes, until the lemon slices have become translucent. Allow to cool, then transfer to a container and place in the fridge.

For the crab, mix the brown crab meat with the mayonnaise and lemon juice, then fold through the white crab meat. Season to taste. Using two large spoons, shape into four large quenelles and set one on each plate.

Very finely slice the fennel. Drain the pickled pears and slice them. Mix the pears with the lemon confit, sliced fennel, frisée and some baby cress and dress on the plates alongside the crab. Serve immediately.

21

· DEVILLED SARDINES ·

Sardines were first eaten in England in the early 15th century.
It is thought that the name of these small oily fish might come
from the Italian island of Sardinia, because they were once
abundant in the local waters there.

Serves 4

100g butter
15g caster sugar
15g English mustard powder
15g cayenne pepper
15g paprika
65ml red wine vinegar
15g salt
15g black peppercorns, finely ground
2 tbsp vegetable oil
8 fresh sardines, gutted and cleaned

Melt the butter, then pour into a bowl. Add the sugar, mustard powder, spices, vinegar, salt and pepper and mix well to make a paste.

Heat a large frying pan with the vegetable oil until almost smoking. Liberally brush the sardines with the devil paste, then fry for 4–6 minutes, until cooked through and a deep reddy brown on both sides. Serve hot.

·CHILLED YELLOW HEIRLOOM· TOMATO SOUP

In the restaurant we call this 'chilled tomato soup', so our guests get a surprise when a bowl of yellow liquid turns up. With a slightly more delicate flavour than the red variety, yellow tomatoes add something a little different. An heirloom tomato is a variety that has been passed down, generation to generation, due to its beneficial characteristics.

Serves 4

500g very ripe, yellow heirloom
tomatoes (any variety), chopped
1 shallot, peeled and finely sliced
1 clove garlic, peeled and finely sliced
50ml Chardonnay or white wine vinegar
a squeeze of lemon juice
1 tbsp blossom honey
500ml vegetable stock
1 tsp salt
1 stalk lemongrass, finely sliced
white pepper to taste

Combine all of the ingredients in a non-reactive bowl and leave to macerate overnight in a cool place, or for 2 days if possible.

Blitz everything together in a blender, then pass through a fine sieve. Taste and adjust the flavour with more salt and vinegar if needed. Serve chilled.

Note: Try this in a glass with a shot of vodka added, for a refreshing Yellow Mary.

· YORKSHIRE FISHCAKES ·
WITH PICKLED CUCUMBER AND DILL MAYONNAISE

Unlike most fishcakes, these contain no potato and instead
are packed with fish. The pickled cucumber adds a delightful
freshness to complement the rich, tasty fishcakes.

Serves 4

250ml milk
½ onion, peeled and finely chopped
1 bay leaf
250g undyed smoked haddock fillet
20g unsalted butter
25g plain flour, plus extra for coating
1 tbsp chopped chives
1 tbsp chopped parsley leaves
grated zest and juice of ¼ lemon
1 hard-boiled free-range egg, grated
1 tbsp capers, chopped
1 free-range egg, well beaten
100g panko breadcrumbs
oil for frying

Pickled cucumber
1 large cucumber
1 tbsp salt
50ml Chardonnay vinegar
1 tsp icing sugar

Mayonnaise
2 free-range egg yolks
½ tsp Dijon mustard
½ tsp made English mustard
2 tbsp white wine vinegar
50ml olive oil
150ml vegetable oil
2 tbsp finely chopped dill
salt and white pepper to taste

Put the milk, onion and bay leaf in a saucepan. Add the
haddock and bring to a simmer, then poach until just cooked.
Remove the fish and peel off the skin, if necessary, then set
aside. Strain and reserve the milk.

Melt the butter in a saucepan and stir in the flour to form
a roux. Add the poaching milk, a ladleful at a time, whisking
continuously, until you have a thick white sauce (you may not
need all of the milk). Cook, stirring, for a few minutes, then
season well and remove from the heat.

Flake the fish and add to the sauce along with the herbs,
lemon zest and juice, hard-boiled egg and capers. Mix gently
together. When cool, roll in clingfilm into a thick sausage
shape. Chill for 1 hour to firm up.

For the pickled cucumber, use a peeler to peel thin strips
lengthways from the cucumber, stopping when you get to the
seeds. Put the strips in a colander, sprinkle with the salt and
leave for 5 minutes, then rinse and dry well. Mix the vinegar
and sugar in a bowl, add the cucumber and pickle for 1 hour.

To make the mayonnaise, whisk together the egg yolks,
mustards and vinegar in a bowl until well combined, then
slowly trickle in the mixed oils, whisking all the time, until
thick in consistency. Season to taste and mix in the dill.

Unwrap the fish 'sausage' and cut across into 2.5cm-thick
cakes. Dip in flour, then into beaten egg and finally into the
breadcrumbs to coat evenly. If you want to deep-fry the fish
cakes, heat a deep pan of oil to 165°C and fry them for 3–4
minutes, until golden brown all over. Alternatively, shallow-
fry for about 2 minutes on each side. Serve hot on a bed of
pickled cucumber with dollops of mayonnaise around.

· 'POTTED' SHRIMPS ·

The traditional way of making potted shrimps is with
Morecambe Bay brown shrimps, mace, clarified butter and
cayenne pepper, set in small ramekins with a layer of butter
on top. For our menu, we broke down the elements of
the classic dish and created a new take.

Serves 4

100g soft unsalted butter
5g ground mace
pinch of cayenne pepper
1 tbsp Madeira
grated zest and juice of ½ lemon
500g peeled and cooked
Morecambe Bay brown shrimps
Maldon sea salt

To serve
8 very thin slices day-old bread, frozen
and then cut into quarters
olive oil

Put the butter in a medium-sized bowl and beat until light
and fluffy (use a hand-held electric mixer if you wish). Add
the mace, cayenne, Madeira, lemon zest and juice, and sea salt
to taste. Beat well. Fold in the shrimps. Check the seasoning,
adding more salt if necessary. Cover and keep in a cool place.

Preheat the oven to 180°C/350°F/gas mark 4. Spread out the
frozen pieces of bread on a baking tray, drizzle over some
olive oil and sprinkle with salt. Toast in the oven until lightly
golden, then leave to cool.

Spoon the shrimp mix into a serving bowl and serve with the
toasts on the side. Perfect with the Queen's favourite tipple
– a martini with a twist of lemon, shaken not stirred.

· WARM JERSEY ROYAL SALAD ·
WITH SMOKED BACON AND THYME

The Jersey Royal potato was discovered in 1878 by a farmer on the island of Jersey. He found two unknown potatoes in his field, which he cut into pieces and planted, thus beginning the production of this special potato. Jerseys have a brief, but highly anticipated, season each year from the beginning of April. Earthy and creamy, their unique taste is due in part to the seaweed used as fertilizer.

Serves 4

500g Jersey Royal potatoes (as similar in size as possible), scrubbed well
200g good-quality smoked bacon lardons
Maldon sea salt

Mayonnaise
2 free-range egg yolks
200ml vegetable oil
1 tbsp thyme leaves
grated zest and juice of 1 lemon
1 tsp Dijon mustard
1 tsp cider vinegar
½ tsp salt

Put the potatoes in a pan of salted cold water and bring to the boil. Cook until almost tender, then drain in a colander. Cool under running cold water for 1 minute before setting aside.

For the mayonnaise, place the yolks in a blender and blitz until slightly paler in colour. With the machine running, very slowly drizzle in half of the oil through the feed tube. Add the thyme leaves, then continue to blend, drizzling in the remaining oil. Add the rest of the ingredients and adjust the seasoning, if necessary.

Fry the bacon lardons in a hot pan, retaining the fat that has rendered from them.

Gently break open the potatoes with your hands and arrange on a platter. Scatter the bacon lardons and bacon fat over the potatoes, then sprinkle lightly with sea salt. Dollop the mayonnaise on top and serve immediately.

· SUMMER GARDEN SALAD ·

British summer produce cannot be beaten and needs very little to complement it when it is fresh and ripe. The saltiness of goat's cheese brings out the best of the different textures of the vegetables here.

Serves 4

400g mixed summer vegetables
(green beans, podded fresh peas, podded
and skinned broad beans, prepared
baby globe artichokes, broccoli florets)
4 tbsp extra virgin olive oil
1 tbsp Chardonnay vinegar
200g goat's cheese – try Childwickbury
(from Childwickbury Estate, Hertfordshire)
1 punnet or bag pea shoots
leaves from ¼ bunch of basil

Blanch the vegetables separately (broccoli last as it will leave a residue in the water): bring a large pan of salted water to the boil, then add the vegetable and cook until it is just tender but still retains a small bite. Remove using a slotted spoon or sieve and plunge into iced water to cool quickly. Drain well and set on a tray lined with kitchen paper to remove any excess moisture.

Put the vegetables in a large bowl. Whisk together the olive oil and vinegar, then pour over the vegetables and season well. Toss to coat. Lay out four plates, or one large serving plate, and arrange the vegetables and cheese along the centre. Garnish with the pea shoots and basil leaves.

· CULLEN SKINK ·

Originating from the fishing village of Cullen, in Moray on the
north-east coast of Scotland, this is a thick, sustaining soup
made with potato, smoked haddock and milk.

Serves 4

50g butter
2 large onions, peeled and finely sliced
3 cloves garlic, peeled and finely sliced
¼ bunch of thyme, firmly tied with string
2 bay leaves
1 litre chicken or vegetable stock
1 litre milk
*2 large floury potatoes, peeled
and finely sliced*
200g smoked haddock fillet
*hot crushed, boiled potatoes mixed
with chopped chives, to serve*

Heat the butter in a large saucepan. Add the onions, garlic
and herbs, and season well. Cook over a low heat for about
15 minutes, ensuring the onions do not brown by adding
a little stock now and again to keep the temperature low.

When the onions are beginning to break down, add the
remaining stock and half of the milk. Bring just to the boil.
Add the potatoes and simmer gently until they are cooked
through. Add half of the haddock to the soup and cook for
a further 5 minutes, then remove the pan from the heat.
Peel any skin from the haddock.

Pour the remaining milk into another saucepan and bring up
to a gentle simmer. Add the remaining haddock and gently
poach for about 5 minutes, until cooked through. Drain the
haddock in a sieve set over a bowl so you retain the milk;
remove any skin from the haddock and set aside in a warm
place. Strain the poaching milk into the soup. Discard the
thyme and bay leaf, then pour into a blender and blitz until
smooth. Pass through a sieve into a clean pan.

Reheat the soup and check the seasoning and consistency.
If it is a bit too thick, add more stock or milk; if it is too
thin, simmer gently for 10 minutes to reduce. Flake the
poached haddock into warmed bowls and add some hot
crushed potatoes. Ladle the soup over at the table.

· DORSET SNAILS ·
WITH BONE MARROW AND TOAST

Snails have become more popular in the last few years, with a snail farm now functioning in Dorset, established in 2006 (check our Suppliers page for further details). It's worth making a lot more roasted garlic purée than you need for this dish as it can be kept in the fridge for 1–2 months; add it to soups or use on cooked meats or mushrooms on toast.

Serves 4

50g butter
20 snails (purchased ready-cooked)
1 tbsp chopped parsley
8 x 8cm-long pieces marrow bone, cut horizontally (ask your butcher to cut the bones for you)
4 slices hot toast

Roasted garlic purée
3 bulbs garlic
1 tbsp vegetable oil
½ tsp salt, plus more if needed
freshly ground black pepper to taste

Begin by making the roasted garlic purée. Preheat the oven to 180°C/350°F/gas mark 4. Slice the tip off each garlic bulb, then place them on a sheet of foil. Drizzle over the oil and sprinkle with the salt. Wrap up in the foil and place in the oven to roast for 30 minutes, until golden. Squeeze the soft garlic flesh from the clove skins into a bowl, then push the flesh through a fine sieve. Season to taste and set aside. Leave the oven on.

Heat a saucepan and add the butter. Add the snails, season well and heat through. Mix in the parsley. Remove from the heat and keep warm.

Heat an ovenproof frying pan on the hob until very hot, then sear the marrow in the centre of the bones until nicely browned. Spread a little of the roasted garlic purée over the marrow, then transfer the frying pan to the oven to cook for 4 minutes.

Arrange the toast on the plates with the marrow bones. Place the snails and small spoonfuls or quenelles of the roasted garlic purée on top, then spoon over the parsley butter. Serve immediately.

29

· KENTISH COBNUTS ·
WITH MUSHROOMS AND SPICE

The cobnut is a cultivated hazelnut that has been grown in Kent since the 1830s. Cobnuts are quite time-consuming to prepare, so if you are short on time you can substitute shelled hazelnuts, although cobnuts have a milkier and fresher taste and a lighter texture than hazelnuts. This is an interesting dish that is great served with fish or chicken, or just on its own.

Serves 4

1 cinnamon stick, crushed
2 star anise, crushed
5 black peppercorns, crushed
2 cloves, crushed
25g butter
400g mixed mushrooms, chopped
100g shelled fresh cobnuts, sliced

Heat a small pan and dry fry the spices until fragrant. Add the butter and allow to foam, then strain the spiced butter through a fine sieve into a frying pan.

Heat the spiced butter again until foaming, then add the mushrooms, seasoning well. Cook, stirring occasionally, until the mushrooms are browned and the liquid they have exuded has evaporated. Add the cobnuts and cook until lightly toasted, stirring.

Serve with your favourite bread or new potatoes.

30

· BACON OLIVES ·
WITH ENDIVE SALAD

Beef Olives is a traditional 16th-century Scottish dish which, despite the name, does not contain any olives. This is a pork version where the 'olives' are sliced and pan-fried. The endive salad is a great partner for the savoury, meaty olives.

Serves 4

Bacon olives
1 tsp chopped sage
1 tsp chopped thyme leaves
250g good-quality pork sausage meat
5 rashers good-quality streaky bacon
vegetable oil, for frying

Salad
1 tbsp grain mustard
1 tbsp clear honey
1 tbsp white wine vinegar
100ml vegetable oil
2 white endives (chicory),
separated into leaves

Mix the sage, thyme and three turns of the peppermill into the sausage meat. Roll the meat in clingfilm to create a large sausage shape approximately 5cm in diameter. Tie the ends of the clingfilm tightly, then chill to set the shape.

Lay the bacon rashers vertically on a large sheet of clingfilm, in one layer but slightly overlapping them. Carefully unwrap the sausage meat roll and lay it horizontally across the bacon. Wrap up the sausage meat in the bacon, then continue rolling in the clingfilm to make a tight roll. Secure the ends of this ballotine tightly by tying up the excess clingfilm or tie with string.

Bring some water to the boil in a steamer. Add the ballotine, cover and steam for 25 minutes. Allow to cool, then place in the fridge to chill and set.

To make the honey mustard dressing, whisk together the mustard, honey and vinegar, then gradually add the oil, whisking well. Season to taste.

Slice the ballotine into rounds about 3cm thick. Fry these 'olives' in a hot pan with a little oil until lightly browned all over. Divide the bacon olives among the plates, place the endive leaves on top and drizzle over the vinaigrette. Serve hot.

31

LONDON PARTICULAR SOUP ·

In an article in the *New York Times* in 1871, the thick, heavy fog that
used to descend on London was described as being akin to 'pea soup'.
When the fog was particularly bad it came to be called a 'pea souper',
and in reverse pea and ham soup was named 'London Particular'.

Serves 4

1 x 200g smoked bacon joint, on the bone
200g yellow split peas, soaked overnight
and drained

Stock
¼ bunch of parsley
¼ bunch of thyme
1 onion, peeled and quartered
1 carrot, peeled and halved
1 stick celery
1 star anise
½ bulb garlic
6 white peppercorns
2 litres water

Place all the ingredients for the stock in a large saucepan.
Add the bacon joint. Bring to the boil, then turn down
the heat and simmer gently for 1 hour, until the bacon
is cooked through. Lift out the bacon. Remove the bone
carefully and pick off the meat in small chunks; set aside.
Strain the stock and return to the pan.

Place the yellow peas in a pan of cold water and bring to
the boil. Boil for 2 minutes, then drain and rinse well. Add
to the stock and simmer gently until the peas are tender.

Scoop out half of the peas and blitz to a purée in a blender
or food processor, then return to the pan. Add the bacon
pieces. Reheat the soup. Check for seasoning and adjust
if necessary, then serve hot.

32

· WHITLEY 'GOOSE' ·

This is a traditional dish from Whitley Bay on the coast near Newcastle-upon-Tyne. Being deliciously creamy, it is great with cold meats and crusty bread.

Serves 4–6

4 onions, peeled and left whole
110g Cheddar cheese, grated
450ml single cream
10g butter
salt and freshly ground black pepper

Put the onions in a saucepan and cover with lightly salted water. Bring to the boil, then boil for 15–20 minutes, until the onions are tender. Drain well and allow to cool a little.

Preheat the grill. Chop the onions roughly and mix with half of the cheese, the cream and some pepper. Taste and add salt if needed. Butter an ovenproof dish and pour in the onion mix. Top with the remaining cheese. Grill until the cheese has melted and the top is dark golden brown. Allow to cool, then place in the fridge to set before serving.

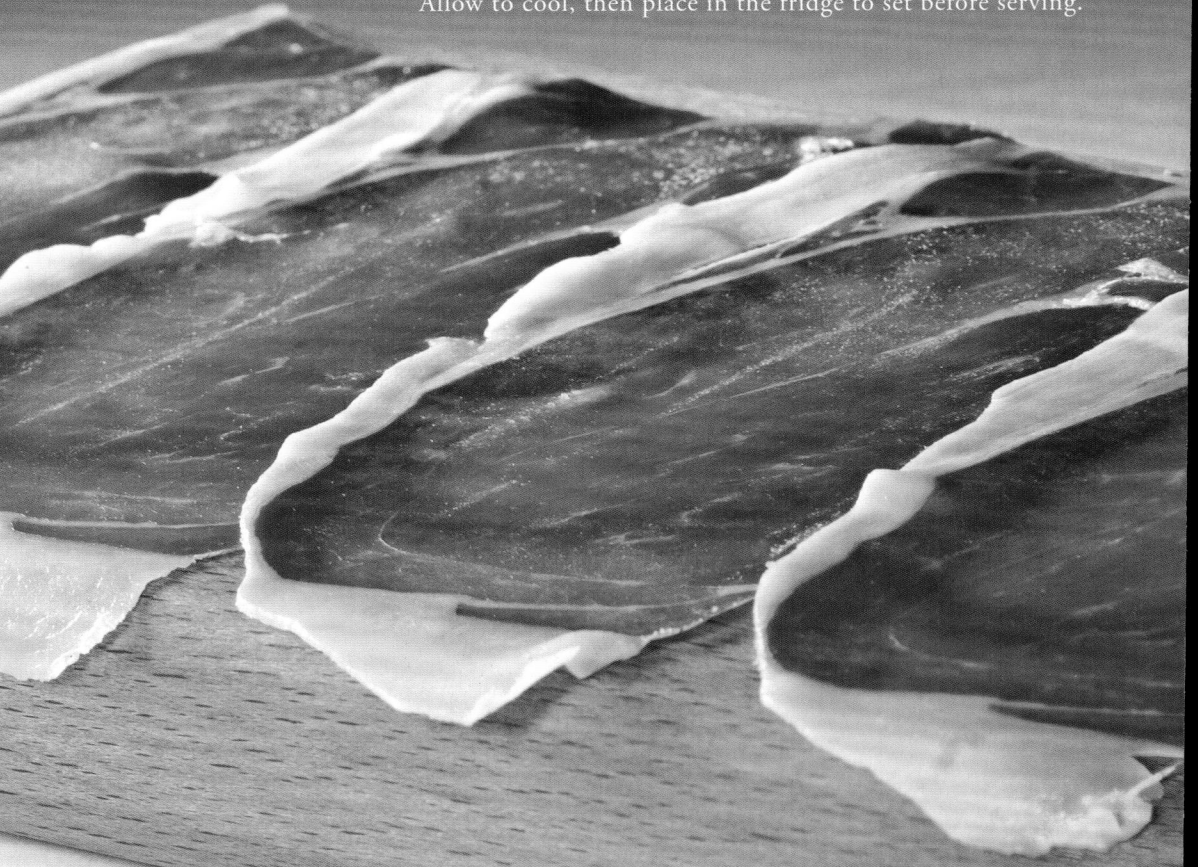

33

· QUINCE ·
WITH ARDRAHAN CHEESE

A semi-soft cheese made from the milk of Freisian cows, Ardrahan
is creamy, earthy and slightly nutty. It is produced on a small farm
in Kanturk, County Cork, Ireland. If unavailable, try a British
cheese similar to the French Livarot or Munster.

Serves 4

*1 large quince, peeled, cored
and cut into eighths
4 tbsp your favourite honey
¼ bunch of thyme
200g Ardrahan cheese (or other washed-rind,
semi-strong cheese), sliced
Maldon sea salt*

Preheat the oven to 160°C/325°F/gas mark 3. Toss the
quince with the honey, thyme and sea salt in a small baking
dish. Cover with foil and bake for 30 minutes, until tender.

Arrange the quince in a small gratin dish. Top with the
cheese, then put back in the oven for a few minutes, until
the cheese has melted. Serve with your favourite bread or
cheese biscuits.

34

· LINCOLNSHIRE HASLET ·

A jazzed-up version of a wonderfully savoury meat loaf,
this is great served with good bread and a glass of wine.

Makes 1 terrine (12 slices)

25g butter
2 onions, peeled and finely sliced
200g boneless pork belly
200g boneless pork shoulder
200g pork liver
60g sliced lardo
60g fresh white breadcrumbs
leaves from ¼ bunch of sage, finely chopped
1 tsp grated allspice
a little oil for frying

Heat a medium-sized frying pan with the butter. When foaming, add the onions with a good pinch of salt. Cook over a moderate heat until the onions are soft and nicely browned. Remove from the heat and set aside.

Mince together the pork belly, shoulder and liver on the coarsest setting on the mincer. You can also use a food processor to do this but take care not to make a purée/paste.

Preheat the oven to 120°C/240°F/gas mark ½. Line a 24 x 10cm terrine mould with the lardo, placing the slices side by side across the width and leaving the ends hanging over the rim of the mould so you can later fold them back on top of the mix.

Mix together the meat, breadcrumbs, onions, sage, allspice and some salt and pepper. Fry a little of the mix to check the seasoning; adjust if necessary. Pack the mix into the lined terrine mould, then fold over the ends of the lardo slices. Wrap the mould completely in foil, then set it in a bain marie or roasting tin half filled with hot water.

Place in the oven and cook for about 1 hour, until the core temperature of the loaf reaches 64°C; check this using a probe instant-read thermometer. Remove from the bain marie and unwrap the foil. Set something heavy on top of the haslet that will press it evenly. Allow to cool, then place in the fridge and chill overnight before slicing to serve. The terrine can be kept for 7 days (store it in the fridge).

em fat and I'll capture them scrawny,
raggle-foot Mulligatawny,
animal fast as the wind,
g sands of the Desert of Zind.
that the brave chieftains ride
o fast to find some place to hide.
for my zoo

· QUAIL MULLIGATAWNY ·

Mulligatawny – literally 'pepper water' in Tamil – refers to a curry-based soup, similar to dhal, that is traditionally made using lamb. Our version is a sweet and spicy soup topped with crisp pieces of quail. The word 'mulligatawny' can be applied to other things too, as it is amusingly in Dr Seuss's book *If I Ran the Zoo*.

Serves 4

25g butter
2 onions, peeled and chopped
1 Granny Smith apple, peeled and grated
2 tbsp mild curry powder
2 tbsp plain flour
300ml chicken stock
1 x 400ml tin coconut milk
100g peeled sweet potato,
cut into 1cm dice
50g Puy lentils, cooked
coriander cress, to garnish

Quails

1 litre chicken stock
¼ bunch of thyme, tied together with string
3 cloves garlic, peeled and lightly smashed
4 quails
2 tbsp vegetable oil
25g unsalted butter

Melt the butter in a saucepan and add the onions and apple with a pinch of salt. Cook, without colouring, for 3–4 minutes, until they begin to soften. Add the curry powder and flour and cook for 2 minutes, stirring well. Pour in the stock and scrape the bottom of the pan with a wooden spoon to remove the sediment. Simmer for 2 minutes, then pass through a fine sieve into a clean saucepan. Add the coconut milk and sweet potato and simmer for about 10 minutes, until the sweet potato is cooked and the soup is thick. Add the cooked lentils and heat through. Season to taste.

While the soup is simmering, prepare the quails. Place the chicken stock, thyme and garlic in a pan over a moderate heat and bring to a simmer. Add the quails and simmer for 2–3 minutes. Remove the quails with a slotted spoon and drain on kitchen paper. When cool enough to handle, use a sharp knife to carefully cut the quail breasts away from the bone in one piece, and take the legs off.

Heat a frying pan until hot, then add the oil and butter. Once the butter is foaming, season the quail breasts and legs and place them, skin-side down, in the pan. Fry for 3–5 minutes, until there is moderate resistance when the thickest part of the breast is squeezed (or until completely cooked through and firm if you prefer) and the legs are crisp. Remove the quail pieces from the pan and leave to rest in a warm place for 5 minutes.

To serve, spoon lentils and sweet potato into the bottom of each dish and place the quail legs on top followed by the quail breasts. Ladle over the soup. Garnish each serving with coriander cress (or chopped coriander).

·HARROGATE LOAF·

This terrine of veal, pork and chicken livers, wrapped in bacon, hails from the town of Harrogate in Yorkshire. It is great served with a dark fruit chutney and your favourite crusty bread or, alternatively, a salad of parsley, shallot rings and capers.

Makes 1 terrine (12 slices)

150ml port
150ml Madeira
150ml brandy
25g butter
1 onion, peeled and finely diced
2 cloves garlic, peeled and crushed
leaves from ½ bunch of thyme
300g boneless veal shoulder
150g streaky bacon
125g pork fat
100g chicken livers
75g shelled green pistachios (unsalted)
a little vegetable oil
125g rashers streaky bacon,
for lining the tin

Place the port, Madeira and brandy in a saucepan. Bring to a simmer and reduce by about three-quarters to a thick syrup. Set aside.

Heat the butter in a frying pan and, when foaming, add the onion, garlic, thyme and some seasoning. Cook until the onion is soft. Set aside.

Preheat the oven to 85°C/185°F/lowest gas mark.

Mince the veal shoulder, bacon, pork fat and chicken livers using a mincer or food processor, and mix together in a bowl. Add the alcohol reduction and mix well, then add the cooked onions, pistachios, 1 teaspoon salt and a good amount of black pepper. Fry a little of the mix in hot oil to check the seasoning – add more salt if necessary.

Line a 24 x 10cm terrine mould with the streaky bacon rashers, laying them crossways and letting the ends hang over the sides of the mould. Pack in the veal and bacon mix. Fold the bacon rashers over to cover the top, then wrap the entire mould tightly in foil. Set the mould in a bain marie or roasting tin half filled with hot water and place in the oven. Cook for 2 hours, topping up the water as necessary.

Remove from the oven and leave to cool. Set a weight on top (preferably something heavy that will fit inside the mould to cover the terrine completely) in order to press it. Chill overnight before serving, in slices. (The terrine can be kept in the fridge for up to 5 days.)

·MUSHROOMS ON SIPPETS·

Sippets, which are pieces of dry bread toasted and topped with
a moist savoury mix, originated in Elizabethan times as a good
use for day-old bread. For this dish you can use whatever
mushrooms are best in season at the time.

Serves 4

400g mixed mushrooms
2 tbsp vegetable oil
½ tsp salt
splash of red wine
50ml beef stock
25g butter
1 clove garlic, peeled and crushed
1 tsp picked thyme leaves
1 tsp chopped parsley
4 slices day-old bread – we use our
Dyett Bread (see page 216)

Ensure the mushrooms are cleaned well, then cut them into
pieces of similar size, so they will cook at the same speed.

Heat a large frying pan with the oil. When almost smoking,
add the mushrooms and salt and brown well. Add the red
wine and cook for 1 minute, then add the beef stock and cook
until it has almost all evaporated. Add the butter, garlic and
herbs and cook for a further 2 minutes, stirring well. Remove
from the heat and keep hot.

Toast the bread. Spoon the mushrooms on top and serve.

MAIN EVENT

The inspiration for the dishes in this chapter has come partly from perusing old English recipe books, such as Mrs Beeton's, but also from my own knowledge of what people like to cook, and what they like to eat. There are some real comfort foods here, such as Lancashire Hotpot and Gower Peninsula Fisherman's Stew, as well as a few great pies, all perfect when the weather is cold and grey. There are also lighter main dishes for warmer times of year.

Using top-quality ingredients to make any of them is, of course, essential. This quote from Mrs Beeton sums up my view: 'Good [shopping] is as important as good cooking, for however efficient and painstaking a cook may be, she can have little success if the ingredients she has to work with are of poor quality.'

38

· MRS BEETON'S · BARBECUE CHICKEN

This dish is derived from a barbecue sauce recipe in Mrs Beeton's *Book of Household Management*. In her book she advises how to run a household (from managing servants to making home-made furniture polish) as well as how to feed your family, very well. An amazing woman who, with five children, achieved so much before her early death at the age of 27.

Serves 4–6

*4 baby chickens, 400–500g each,
spatchcocked*

Barbecue sauce
*50g tomato purée
1 tbsp black treacle
1 tbsp Worcestershire sauce
½ tsp sweet smoked paprika
½ tsp hot smoked paprika
juice of ½ lemon
1 clove garlic, peeled and finely chopped
pinch of salt
freshly ground black pepper to taste*

Mix together all of the ingredients for the barbecue sauce. Rub half of the sauce all over the chickens in a bowl or plastic bag, then cover and leave to marinate in the fridge overnight.

Prepare a charcoal fire in a barbecue, or heat a chargrill pan, and preheat the oven to 180°C/350°F/gas mark 4. Spread the rest of the barbecue sauce over the chickens, then cook over the hot coals, or chargrill, until crisp and a little charred on both sides. Transfer the chickens to a roasting tin and finish cooking in the oven for 8–10 minutes.

39

· LEEK CRUMBLE ·

This is a good dish to encourage children to learn to love vegetables.
A savoury version along the lines of apple crumble, it contains
cheese and thyme to boost the flavour.

Serves 4

4 leeks, white part mainly, sliced
into 2cm rounds
25g butter

Sauce
50g butter
50g plain flour
200ml chicken stock
200ml milk
50g smoked cheese, grated
1 tbsp grain mustard
1 tsp made English mustard
½ tsp salt

Crumble topping
100g wholemeal flour
100g rolled oats
25g sesame seeds
2 tbsp thyme leaves
½ tsp salt
25g butter
100g Cheddar cheese, grated
1 tsp grain mustard
freshly ground black pepper to taste

Preheat the oven to 180°C/350°F/gas mark 4.

Begin by frying the leeks with the butter in a large frying
pan until lightly coloured and almost cooked. Place in an
ovenproof dish, or four individual dishes, and set aside.

To make the sauce, melt the butter in a saucepan, stir in the
flour and cook for 5 minutes. Add the stock, whisking well,
then add the milk and cook until the sauce is thick, stirring
continuously. Add the smoked cheese, mustards and salt and
mix well. Cover the leeks with the sauce.

For the crumble topping, mix together the flour, oats,
sesame seeds, thyme, salt and some pepper. Rub the butter
into the mix until it resembles crumbs, then add the cheese
and mustard. Spread over the leeks in sauce.

Bake for about 20 minutes, until bubbling and golden.
Serve hot, with a fresh tomato chutney and salad.

40

· RABBIT AND PRAWN PIE ·

Rabbit with prawns may seem odd, but the 'surf and turf' combination works wonderfully well in this pie. Ensure the rabbit legs are cooked gently until tender and that the sauce is rich and flavoursome. Wild rabbit will yield the best flavour but if not available you can use farmed rabbit or chicken.

Makes 1 large pie or 4 small pies

20 raw prawns
4 tbsp vegetable oil
5 wild rabbit legs
100g plain flour
1 medium onion, peeled and finely diced
1 clove garlic, peeled and finely crushed
½ tsp fennel seeds
5 black peppercorns
2 star anise
2 bay leaves
¼ bunch of thyme
½ bunch of tarragon, leaves picked from
half of the sprigs and chopped
1 tbsp tomato purée
250ml white wine
250ml chicken stock
50g unsalted butter
leaves from ¼ bunch of parsley, chopped
1 tsp French mustard
1 tbsp grain mustard

Pastry
200g plain flour
100g cold butter, cubed
½ tsp salt
about 50ml iced water
1 free-range egg yolk, beaten

Peel the prawns and set aside; reserve the heads and shells. Heat a large, deep pan with 2 tablespoons of the vegetable oil. Dust the rabbit legs with salt and half of the flour, then brown well all over in the hot oil. Remove and set aside.

Add the remaining oil to the pan, then sweat the onion until soft, without colouring. Add the prawn heads and shells, the garlic, fennel seeds, peppercorns, star anise, bay leaves, thyme and bunch of tarragon sprigs. Cook for 5 minutes. Stir in the tomato purée and wine and cook for a further 5 minutes. Add half of the chicken stock and bring to the boil, then add the remaining stock and bring up to the boil again. Return the rabbit legs to the pan. Simmer for 1 hour, until the legs are cooked through.

Meanwhile, make the pastry. Combine the flour, butter and salt in a food processor and blitz until the mix resembles breadcrumbs. Add just enough iced water to bind, blitzing briefly to combine. Wrap and leave to rest in the fridge for half an hour before rolling out.

Remove the rabbit legs from the cooking liquor and allow to cool slightly, then remove the meat from the bone, keeping it in good-size chunks. Set aside. Strain the cooking liquor through a fine sieve into a bowl, pressing well on all the flavourings (if you have a good blender, blend half of the cooking liquor, then mix it with the rest of the liquor before straining).

Melt the butter in a saucepan, add the remaining 50g flour and mix well. Add a little of the strained cooking liquor and whisk well, then add the remaining liquid. Bring to the boil and simmer gently for 5 minutes. Taste and adjust the seasoning, then finish with the chopped parsley and tarragon and the mustards. Add the prawns and rabbit chunks and mix into the sauce. Set aside.

Preheat the oven to 180°C/350°F/gas mark 4.

Roll out the pastry on a lightly floured surface to 4mm thick and cut to the required shape to make a lid for your pie dish or dishes – for a large pie use a 22cm diameter dish that is 4cm deep, or for individual pies use four 11 x 5cm oval dishes that are 3.5cm deep. Spoon the filling into the pie dish(es). Brush the rim of the pie dish with egg yolk, then place the pastry lid on top and press to the rim to seal. Brush the pastry lid with egg yolk, then bake for about 20 minutes, until golden brown. Allow to rest for 5 minutes before serving.

41

·LONDON PRIDE BATTERED COD·
WITH MUSHY PEA 'MAYONNAISE'

We have served this dish at the restaurant since we opened. We set out to make it slightly different from the norm, so instead of serving mushy peas, mayonnaise and vinegar with the fish and chips, we combined all three accompaniments in one. London Pride is a rich ale that is the perfect addition to the batter.

Serves 4–6

2 tbsp rock salt
4 x 150g pieces of cod fillet
oil for deep frying

'Mayonnaise'
1 x 300g tin Harry Ramsden's mushy peas
100ml light olive oil
2 tbsp Chardonnay vinegar
½ tsp salt

Batter
50g cornflour
100g plain flour
½ tsp salt
250ml London Pride lager

To make the 'mayonnaise', put the mushy peas in a blender and blitz until smooth, then gradually blend in the oil. Finish with the vinegar and salt. Set aside.

Sprinkle the rock salt over the cod and leave for about 10 minutes, then rinse off and pat dry.

Make the batter while the cod is being salted. Sift the cornflour, plain flour and salt into a bowl and whisk in enough beer to make a thick batter.

Heat oil in a deep-fat fryer to 165°C. Taking one piece at a time, coat the fish generously in the batter, then fry until golden on both sides and cooked through (use a skewer to check that the centre of the fish is hot). Drain on kitchen paper.

Serve hot with the 'mayonnaise' and chunky chips.

42

· BEEF FAGGOTS ·

Historically, a 'faggot' was a bundle of sticks, and the term eventually came to be applied to a bundle, or meatball, of offal and meat – the first appearance of this usage in an English dictionary was in 1851. Faggots had their greatest popularity during the period of Second World War rationing as they were a great way of using less desirable cuts of meat.

Mix together all of the ingredients for the faggots. (Or, if you have a mincer, mince them together, using chuck steak instead of mince. You could also use a food processor, as long as you keep the meat chunky.) Fry a little of the mix to check the seasoning; adjust if necessary. Shape into 12 balls and chill in the fridge until firm.

Heat some oil in a frying pan and fry the faggots, in batches, until browned all over. Set aside.

Preheat the oven to 150°C/300°F/gas mark 2. Coat the onion slices in flour, then place in the bottom of a flameproof casserole with the garlic and thyme. Combine the remaining gravy ingredients in a saucepan and bring to the boil. Place the faggots on top of the onions, then pour the boiling liquid over the top. Cover with a lid or foil and bake for 2 hours. Serve hot.

Makes 12

Faggots
450g beef mince (or chuck
  steak – see method)
100g calf's liver, finely chopped
100g smoked streaky bacon, finely chopped
1 onion, peeled and finely chopped
leaves from ¼ bunch of thyme, chopped
leaves from ¼ bunch of flat-leaf
  parsley, chopped
2 cloves garlic, peeled and finely chopped
1 tsp dried sage
4 tbsp Worcestershire sauce
1 tbsp grain mustard
100g fresh breadcrumbs (preferably brioche)
1 tsp salt
freshly ground black pepper to taste
oil for frying

Gravy
2 large onions, peeled and sliced
1 tbsp plain flour
3 cloves garlic, peeled and lightly smashed
¼ bunch of thyme sprigs, tied together
250ml beef stock
50ml red wine
4 tbsp Worcestershire sauce
1 tsp Marmite
2 tbsp red wine vinegar

· PORK CHOP AND BBQ RIB ·
WITH APPLE AND ENDIVE

We source our pork for the restaurant from Great Garnetts Farm in Essex. Run by a family who started the farm in the 1970s, the pigs are reared with utmost care to ensure they are happy and healthy, resulting in a flavoursome and tender end product.

Serves 4

30g salt
600ml boiling water
4 pork chops, about 150g each
2 white endives (chicory)
25g unsalted butter
100ml chicken stock

Ribs

1 litre apple juice
1 knob fresh root ginger, peeled
1 red chilli · 2 shallots, peeled
2 cloves garlic, peeled
½ tsp coriander seeds
1 each star anise and cinnamon stick
1 tsp ground allspice
1 tbsp black peppercorns
1 rack of pork spare ribs (about 10 bones)

Barbecue sauce

140g tomato ketchup · 1 tsp black treacle
1 tsp Worcestershire sauce
1 tbsp grain mustard
½ tsp each sweet and hot smoked paprika
dash of Tabasco sauce · juice of ½ lemon
1 clove garlic, peeled and finely chopped

Apple purée

2 Braeburn apples
2 tbsp honey
leaves from 3 sprigs of lemon thyme
1 tbsp vegetable oil

Start with the ribs. Put the apple juice and all the aromatics and flavourings in a pan large enough to hold the rack of ribs. Bring to the boil, then reduce to a gentle simmer. Add the ribs, cover and cook gently for about 2 hours, until the meat is falling off the bone.

Meanwhile, dissolve the salt in the boiling water, then cool. Place the pork chops in a bowl or plastic bag, add the brine and leave in a cool place for 1 hour; drain.

For the barbecue sauce, mix together all the ingredients and set aside.

Preheat the oven to 165°C/325°F/gas mark 3. To make the apple purée, cut the apples into quarters and toss them with the honey, lemon thyme and a good pinch of salt. Place in a small roasting dish with the oil and bake for 20–30 minutes, until soft and golden. Purée in a blender, then pass through a fine sieve into a pan. Leave the oven on.

Remove the rack of ribs from the stock and set aside. Bring the stock to the boil and reduce to a syrup. Strain, then add to the barbecue sauce. Cut the rack into single rib bones and coat in the sauce in an ovenproof dish. Set aside.

Cut the endives lengthways into quarters. Melt the butter in an ovenproof frying pan, add the endive and sear until well coloured all over. Add the chicken stock, then transfer to the oven to finish cooking for 6–8 minutes, until tender.

Meanwhile, chargrill or grill the pork chops until cooked to your liking (best served slightly pink); heat the ribs in the oven; and warm the apple purée. Serve everything hot.

· QUEEN ANNE'S · ARTICHOKE TART

This recipe is adapted from John Nott's cookery book, *The Cooks and Confectioners Dictionary, or the Accomplish'd Housewifes Companion*, published in 1723. Nott was cook to the Duke of Bolton and his book of French-inspired recipes was very popular at the time.

Serves 4

300g all-butter puff pastry, thawed if frozen
2 free-range egg yolks, beaten

Vinaigrette
100ml extra virgin olive oil
30ml Chardonnay vinegar

Filling
50g butter
1 small leek, white part only, chopped
1 small onion, peeled and sliced
½ tsp salt
1 x 400g jar marinated artichoke hearts, drained well
50ml double cream
1 tbsp each chopped tarragon, chervil and parsley

Roll out the pastry on a floured work surface to 3mm thickness. Transfer to a tray and place in the fridge to relax for 20 minutes. Then cut out two 20cm discs, or eight 12cm discs if you want to make four individual tarts. Cut out the inside of one 20cm disc (or four of the 12cm discs) to create a 2cm wide ring. Brush the edge of the complete pastry disc with beaten egg yolk, then place the ring on top. Transfer to a baking tray lined with baking parchment. Return to the fridge to rest for 20 minutes. Meanwhile, preheat the oven to 180°C/350°F/gas mark 4.

Brush the pastry all over with beaten egg yolk. Set four small, 4cm-deep metal rings at the corners of the baking tray to support another baking tray on top. This will ensure the pastry rises straight up and does not overpuff. Place the double tray in the oven and bake for 15–20 minutes, until the pastry is golden. Remove from the oven and cut out the top layer of the centre of the pastry, which will have risen up, to create a deep cavity in the case. Leave the oven on.

Mix together the ingredients for the vinaigrette with seasoning to taste. Set aside.

Melt the butter in a pan, add the leek, onion and salt, and cook until very soft. Chop half of the artichokes finely, then add to the pan with the cream. Bring to a gentle simmer, stirring well. Purée this mixture in a blender until smooth.

Spoon the hot purée into the tart case, then garnish with the remaining artichokes, cut into wedges. Bake for 8 minutes, until lightly golden. Drizzle the vinaigrette over the top and sprinkle over the herbs. Serve hot.

· LANCASHIRE HOTPOT ·

I grew up in Southport in Lancashire, so this dish reminds me of my childhood. Lamb neck is such a flavoursome cut and creates a fantastic hotpot. The old-fashioned way was to start it in the morning and leave it to cook in a very low oven all day. It made a good nutritious and filling meal for the workers on returning home.

Serves 4

600g boneless lamb neck fillet
(keep the bones for the stock),
cut into 2cm slices
2 tbsp vegetable oil
200g button mushrooms, quartered
2 tbsp plain flour
1 tsp salt
1 tsp ground white pepper
1 onion, peeled and finely sliced
3 large potatoes, peeled and sliced
50g butter, melted

Stock

2 tbsp vegetable oil
1 medium onion, peeled and diced
2 cloves garlic, peeled and crushed
2 tbsp tomato purée
½ tsp cumin seeds
100ml white wine
2 litres chicken or vegetable stock
2 bay leaves
¼ bunch of rosemary
¼ bunch of thyme

First make the stock. Heat the oil in a large saucepan over a moderate heat. Add the onion, garlic, tomato purée and cumin seeds to the pan and lightly caramelize the onion. Add the white wine and reduce to a syrup. Add the stock, lamb bones and herbs to the pan, then cover and allow to simmer gently for 30 minutes. Strain the stock and season with salt, then set aside.

Preheat the oven to 150°C/300°F/gas mark 2. Heat a frying pan with the oil and fry the mushrooms, in batches, until golden, seasoning well. Set aside.

Mix the flour with the salt and white pepper, then use this to coat the lamb fillet slices. Make alternate layers of lamb, mushrooms and onion in a baking dish. Pour in enough lamb stock to come up to the level of the ingredients. Mix the potato slices with the melted butter and season well, then arrange over the top in a spiral shape to cover completely (you should have at least a double layer of potato).

Set the dish in a roasting tin to catch any sauce that bubbles over, then bake for 40 minutes, until the lamb is just cooked through. If you like, place the hotpot under the grill to brown the potatoes. Allow to rest for a few minutes before serving.

Note: the hotpot can be made in advance and cooled. Reheat it in a 180°C/350°F/gas mark 4 oven for 20–25 minutes.

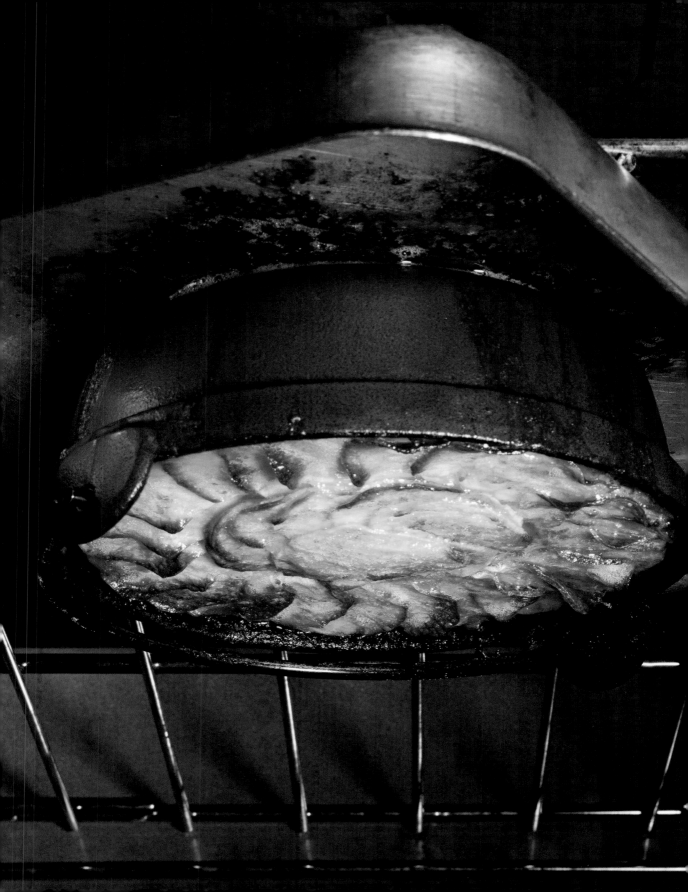

46

MUSHROOM COBBLER

Cobblers originated in the early British colonies in North America. As the settlers were unable to make traditional suet puddings, due to a lack of suitable ingredients and cooking equipment, they covered a stewed filling (sweet or savoury) with a layer of uncooked plain biscuits or dumplings. When fully cooked, the surface resembled a cobbled street, hence the name.

Serves 4

250g flat mushrooms
250g oyster mushrooms
250g Paris Brown mushrooms
4 tbsp vegetable oil
100g baby spinach
50g wild garlic (when in season), shredded

Topping

175g self-raising flour
5g baking powder
30g Cheddar cheese, grated
1 tbsp chopped tarragon
1 tbsp chopped flat-leaf parsley
½ tsp salt
½ tsp black pepper
100g cold butter, grated
2 free-range egg yolks, beaten with
a splash of water, for glazing

Sauce

1 litre milk
1 bay leaf
1 onion, peeled and halved
5 cloves
2 sprigs thyme
75g butter
75g plain flour
100g extra mature Cheddar cheese, grated
grated nutmeg

First make the scone dough for the topping. Mix together the flour, baking powder, Cheddar, herbs, salt and pepper in a bowl. Gently mix in the butter, then add just enough cold water to bring together to a dough. Take care not to over-mix, which would make the scones tough. Rest the dough in the fridge for at least 2 hours.

Roll out the scone dough on a lightly floured surface to 1cm thickness. Cut into 16–24 discs about 4cm in diameter. Cover and keep in the fridge until needed.

Preheat the oven to 180°C/350°F/gas mark 4.

For the sauce, put the milk in a saucepan with the bay leaf, onion, cloves and thyme and bring to a simmer. Remove from the heat and leave to infuse for 30 minutes. Strain the milk. Melt the butter in a clean pan, stir in the flour and cook over a gentle heat for 5 minutes to form a roux. Gradually whisk in the milk, then simmer for 10 minutes. Add the cheese and nutmeg and seasoning to taste. Set aside.

Cut the flat mushrooms into chunky strips; tear the oyster mushrooms into pieces of the same size; and cut the Paris mushrooms into quarters. Fry, in batches, in the oil in a hot pan to colour the mushrooms and evaporate the liquid they exude, seasoning with salt and pepper as you go.

Place all the mushrooms in a large bowl and add the spinach and wild garlic. Stir in enough cheese sauce to coat the mushrooms, then spoon into four individual pie dishes about 10cm in diameter and 7cm deep. Top with the scones and brush them with the egg wash. Bake for 15–20 minutes, until the filling is bubbling and the scones are golden. Serve hot.

· SUMMER THYME ·

Made with fragrant ripe strawberries, fresh thyme, and vodka flavoured with the aromatic fruit feijoa, this cocktail is the essence of summer.

8 strawberries
4 sprigs thyme
80ml Tapatío Anéjo tequila
30ml fresh lime juice
25ml elderflower cordial
20ml 42 Below feijoa vodka
ice cubes

To garnish
1 strawberry, halved
2 sprigs thyme

Muddle the strawberries and thyme with the tequila in a cocktail shaker. Alternatively, use the end of a rolling pin in a larger container to gently pound these ingredients together. Add the lime juice, cordial and vodka, top up with ice and shake for 1 minute. Strain into a jug, then strain a second time into two coupe glasses. Garnish each with half a strawberry on the rim and a thyme sprig curled up the stem of the glass.

9

· SUGAR SYRUP ·

Makes about 200ml

70g caster sugar
30g liquid glucose
200ml water

Combine the ingredients in a pan and bring to the boil, stirring to dissolve the sugar. Remove from the heat and set aside to cool. This can be kept in the fridge in a screwtop jar for 2 weeks.

· GOWER PENINSULA ·
FISHERMAN'S STEW

The Gower Peninsula is located on the coast of South Wales, jutting out into the Bristol Channel. A dish like this was made for the Welsh fishermen who would bring home some of their day's catch in the morning for their wives to cook. The men would go to bed, then get up at suppertime to find a hot fish stew waiting for them.

Serves 4

12 large raw prawns
12 fresh mussels, scrubbed and debearded
2 large potatoes, peeled and
cut into 3cm cubes
8 bulbs baby fennel, halved
12 small scallops (without roe)
400g skinless firm white fish fillets,
such as cod or pollock, cut into
bite-sized pieces
200g skinless salmon or sea trout fillet,
cut into bite-sized pieces

Broth

2 tbsp vegetable oil
1 onion, peeled and halved
2 carrots, peeled and cut across in half
1 bulb garlic, halved horizontally
1 leek, white part only, cut across in half
3 sticks celery, cut across in half
4 tbsp tomato purée
pinch of saffron threads
250ml white wine
¼ bunch of tarragon
¼ bunch of thyme
2 litres chicken stock

Peel the prawns and pull off the heads; set the prawns aside. Rinse the shells and heads. To make the broth, heat the vegetable oil in a large saucepan. When almost smoking add the prawn heads and shells together with the onion, carrots, garlic, leek and celery. Brown well, stirring. Add the tomato purée and saffron, then deglaze with the white wine. When reduced to a syrup, add the herbs and stock and bring to the boil. Simmer for 1 hour.

Pass through a fine sieve into a clean pan, pressing down on the prawn shells and vegetables to extract all the liquid; discard the vegetables and shells. Bring the broth to the boil, then add the mussels. Cover and cook until the shells open. Remove the mussels with a slotted spoon; keep warm.

Strain the broth into another pan to remove any grit from the mussels, then bring back to the boil and adjust the seasoning. Add the potatoes and fennel and cook until almost tender. Add the prawns, scallops and fish, and simmer gently until just cooked. Return the mussels to the stew, then serve.

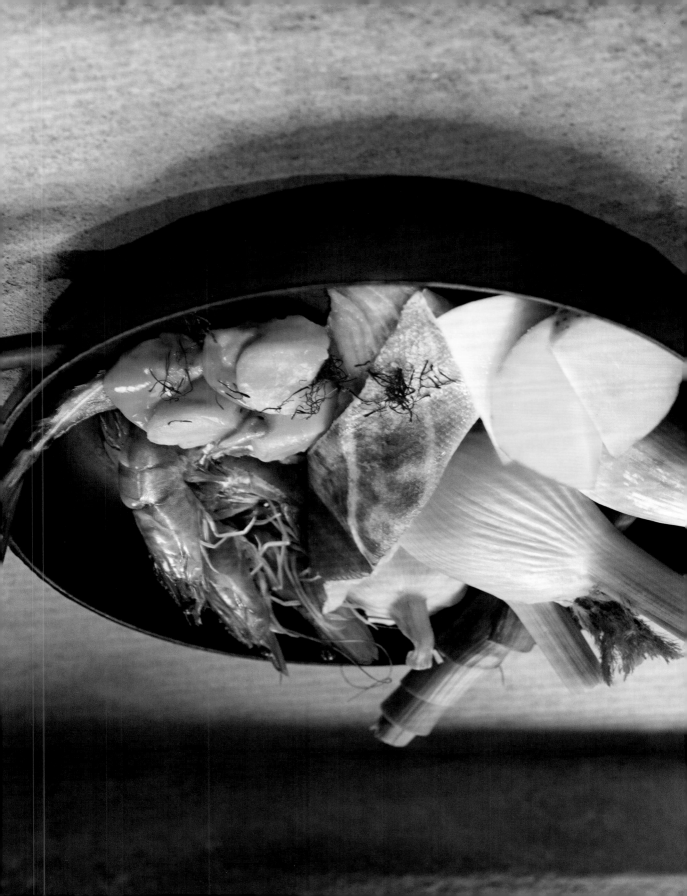

PASTAI COCOS
(COCKLE PIE)

Sweet, salty cockles are combined with ham hock and leeks in this traditional Welsh dish. It is important to use cockles from a reputable supplier to ensure they have as little sand in them as possible.

Makes 1 large pie or 4 small pies

2 smoked ham hocks, soaked in
cold water for 1 hour (change the
water every 15 minutes)
2 leeks, white part only, sliced
into 1.5cm rounds
200ml white wine
1kg cockles, rinsed under running
water for at least 15 minutes
to remove any grit

Ham hock cooking liquor
2 carrots, peeled and cut across in half
1 leek, white part only, cut across in half
6 white peppercorns
1 onion, peeled and halved
2 bay leaves
2 cloves garlic, peeled and lightly smashed

Pastry
200g plain flour
100g butter, cubed
½ tsp salt
about 50ml iced water
1 free-range egg yolk, beaten

Sauce
50g butter
50g plain flour
100ml cream

Begin by cooking the ham hocks. Put all of the ingredients for the cooking liquor in a large saucepan, add the hocks and cover with water. Bring to the boil, then reduce to a simmer. Cook for 3–4 hours, until the bone can be pulled out of the meat. Remove the hocks and set aside.

Strain the ham stock through a fine sieve into a clean saucepan. Bring to the boil, then add the leeks and poach until tender. Drain in a sieve set over a clean saucepan; set the leeks aside. Bring the stock to the boil again and reduce by half, skimming any scum off the top. Meanwhile, break up the meat from the ham hocks, discarding any sinew and keeping the meat in large chunks; set aside.

Bring the white wine to the boil in a saucepan. Add the cockles, cover and steam until the shells have opened. Strain off the wine, reserving it for later. Allow the cockles to cool slightly before removing the flesh from the shells. Set aside.

For the pastry, put the flour, butter and salt into a food processor and blitz until the mix resembles breadcrumbs. Add just enough iced water to bind and process until just combined. Allow to rest for half an hour in the fridge, then roll out to 4mm thickness and cut to the required shape(s) to make a lid for your pie dish or dishes – for a large pie, use a 22cm dish that is 4cm deep; for small pies use four 11 x 5cm oval dishes that are 3.5cm deep.

Preheat the oven to 180°C/350°F/gas mark 4.

Make the sauce while the pastry is resting. Melt the butter in a saucepan, stir in the flour and cook for 3 minutes. Gradually add the white wine from the cockles and cook for 2 minutes. Then stir in 200ml of the ham stock (if it tastes very salty, use half stock and half milk). Cook for 5 minutes, stirring well. Finish with the cream and check the seasoning.

Combine the leeks, cockles, ham and sauce, then spoon into the pie dish. Brush the rim of the dish with egg yolk, then lay the pastry lid on top and press to seal to the rim. Brush the pastry lid with egg yolk. Use the tip of a knife to score lightly with a pattern, if you wish. Bake for 16–20 minutes, until golden brown. Serve hot.

49

· CUMBERLAND SAUSAGES ·
AND MASH

A Cumberland sausage, made with coarsely chopped pork and seasoned generously with both black and white pepper, is traditionally coiled rather than divided into individual lengths. We wanted to serve it in a creative way, so rather than just piling it on a plate, we coiled the sausages in small pans and added gravy, then piped mash on top.

Serves 4

1 large or 4 small rings of good-quality Cumberland sausage

Gravy
2 tbsp vegetable oil
1 onion, peeled and sliced
3 cloves garlic, peeled and lightly smashed
1 tbsp plain flour
250ml beef stock
4 tbsp Worcestershire sauce
1 tbsp red wine vinegar
1 tbsp thyme leaves
pinch of salt

Mash
400g mashing potatoes, peeled and cut to the same size
50g butter
150ml milk or cream
½ tsp salt
2 free-range egg yolks

Preheat the oven to 180°C/350°F/gas mark 4.

For the gravy, heat the oil in a frying pan and fry the onion and garlic until golden. Mix in the flour. Add the rest of the gravy ingredients, stirring well. Bring to the boil, then simmer for 20 minutes, stirring occasionally. Check the seasoning and adjust if necessary.

While the gravy is simmering, make the mash. Place the potatoes in a pan of salted water and bring to the boil. Simmer until tender, then drain well and mash with the butter and milk or cream. Add the salt and egg yolks and mix well. Cover and set aside.

Chargrill, grill or fry the sausage ring(s) to brown on all sides. Place in an appropriate-sized ovenproof dish and cover with the gravy. Spoon or pipe the mash on top to cover completely. Bake for 25 minutes, until the sausage is cooked through. Serve hot, in the dish.

50

· SUFFOLK STEW ·

In Suffolk, stoneground bread and hard Suffolk cheese used to be the staple diet of the outdoor workers. At weekends, though, there would always be a more substantial spread, which is when this rustic stew used to feature. We've added anchovies to enhance the savouriness of the dish.

Serves 4

500g boneless shoulder of mutton, diced into large pieces
1 tsp salt
½ tsp coarsely ground black pepper
2 tbsp plain flour
2 tbsp vegetable oil
1 medium onion, peeled and diced
4 cloves garlic, peeled and lightly smashed
1 carrot, peeled and cut across in half
100g tomato purée
1 tsp cumin seeds, toasted and lightly crushed
250ml white wine
1 litre chicken or vegetable stock
3 bay leaves
½ bunch of rosemary
½ bunch of thyme

1 small tin of good-quality anchovies, drained
100g pearl barley, cooked
100g Puy lentils, cooked

Season the mutton with the salt and pepper and coat in the flour. Heat the oil in a large saucepan over a moderate heat. Add the mutton to the pan and brown well in the hot oil. Remove from the pan and set aside.

Add the onion, garlic, carrot, tomato purée and cumin seeds to the pan and lightly caramelize the vegetables. Pour in the wine and reduce to a syrup, stirring well. Add the stock and herbs and return the mutton to the pan. Bring to the boil, then cover and allow to simmer gently for 45 minutes.

Use a slotted spoon to remove the mutton and set aside. Strain the braising liquor through a fine sieve into a clean pan. Bring to the boil, then add 3 chopped anchovies, the pearl barley and the lentils. Check the seasoning and adjust if necessary. Simmer gently for 5 minutes. Add the mutton and cook for a further 10 minutes. If you wish, stir in more chopped anchovies before serving with some hot mash.

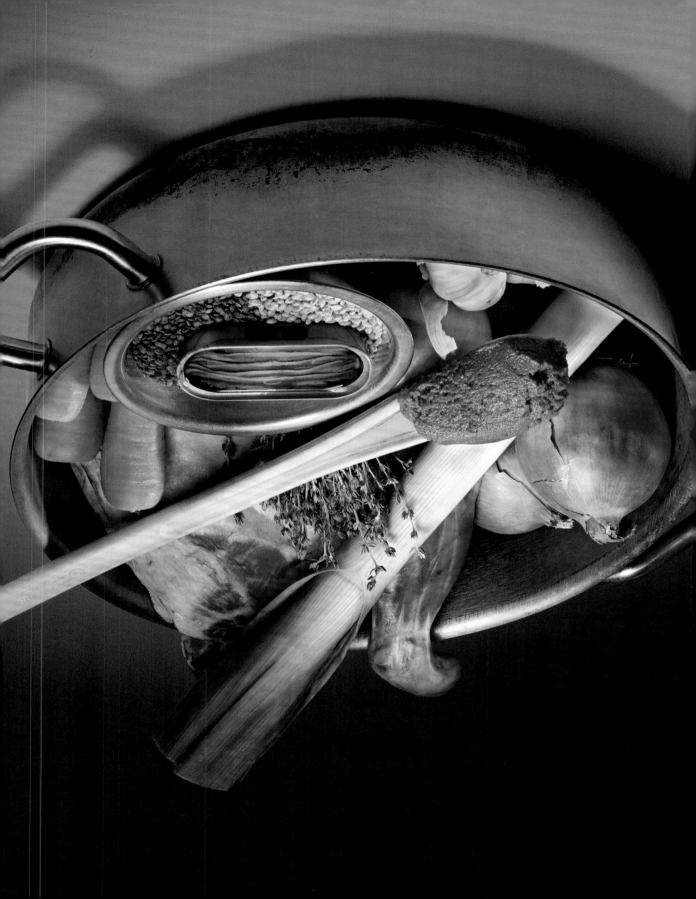

51

· DEVILLED MACKEREL ·
WITH PLUM TOMATO SALAD

Dating back to the 18th century, a 'devil' sauce, or something
devilled, denotes that it is hot and spicy. The UK has a plentiful supply
of wonderful mackerel and when it is fresh its rich flesh works
perfectly with a devil sauce and a sweet tomato salad.

Serves 4

1 tbsp vegetable oil
4 fresh mackerel, gutted and cleaned

Devil sauce
100g butter
1 tbsp treacle
1 tsp made English mustard
½ tsp cayenne pepper
1 tsp smoked paprika
65ml red wine vinegar
1 tsp salt
freshly ground black pepper to taste

Salad
1 tbsp your favourite honey
1 tbsp red wine or sherry vinegar
1 tsp fish sauce
2 tbsp extra virgin olive oil
500g baby plum tomatoes, halved
2 banana shallots, peeled and diced
1 clove garlic, peeled and finely crushed
leaves from ¼ bunch of coriander, chopped

Preheat the oven to 180°C/350°F/gas mark 4.

For the devil sauce, melt the butter in a small pan, then
remove from the heat and stir in the remaining ingredients.

Heat a large ovenproof frying pan with the vegetable oil
until almost smoking. Liberally brush the devil sauce over
the mackerel, then fry until nicely browned on each side.
Transfer to the oven to finish cooking for 6–10 minutes.
Remove and allow to rest for a few minutes.

Meanwhile, make the salad. Mix together the honey,
vinegar, fish sauce and oil. Combine the rest of the
ingredients in a bowl, add the dressing with a good
pinch of salt and fold together.

Serve the fish hot, with the salad.

52

· LAMB SHOULDER ·
ON SIGNS
ON SIPPETS

We've brined the lamb in this recipe as the results are so good –
brining tenderizes the meat while also seasoning it. You just
need to remember to do it the night before.

Serves 4–6

1 x 600–800g boned shoulder of lamb
3 onions, peeled and sliced
¼ bunch of thyme, tied together
with ¼ bunch of rosemary
6 cloves garlic, peeled and cut in half
1 tbsp fennel seeds, toasted
and lightly crushed
1 tsp salt
1 tsp white peppercorns
1 bulb fennel, sliced
1 litre chicken stock

Brine
25g salt
100ml boiling water
5 litres cold water

To serve
4–6 slices day-old bread, lightly toasted
6 tbsp chopped flat-leaf parsley leaves

To make the brine, dissolve the salt in the boiling water
in a large bowl or other large container, then add the cold
water. Immerse the lamb in the brine, cover and leave in the
fridge for 12 hours. Remove the lamb and discard the brine.

Preheat the oven to 150°C/300°F/gas mark 2. Put the sliced
onions, thyme and rosemary bouquet, garlic, fennel seeds,
salt and white peppercorns in a deep ovenproof dish that
will comfortably accommodate the lamb shoulder. Add the
lamb and sliced fennel and pour in the chicken stock to
cover the lamb. Cover the dish with a lid or foil and place
in the oven. Cook for 4–5 hours, until tender.

Lift out the lamb and break up the meat into chunks; keep
hot. Remove the herbs from the cooking liquor. Put a sippet
(a slice of toast) in each deep plate, pile the chunks of lamb
on top and spoon over the onion liquor. Garnish with the
chopped parsley and serve.

· PIGEON IN A PUDDING ·

One of our most popular dishes in the restaurant during the winter months, this is a large Yorkshire pudding filled with a rich, meaty pigeon stew. Brining the pigeon makes it tender and ensures it stays moist throughout the cooking process.

Serves 4

4 wood pigeons
1 tbsp salt
100ml hot water
900ml cold water
2 tbsp vegetable oil
25g butter

Sauce

2 tbsp vegetable oil
1 onion, peeled and sliced
1 carrot, peeled and sliced
1 leek, white part only, sliced
1 clove garlic, peeled and roughly sliced
6 white peppercorns
100ml red wine
¼ bunch of thyme
500ml beef stock

Yorkshire puddings

140g plain flour
200ml milk
4 free-range eggs
½ tsp salt
vegetable oil, for cooking

250g button mushrooms, quartered
100g smoked streaky bacon, diced
2 tbsp vegetable oil
leaves from ¼ bunch of flat-leaf parsley, chopped

Take the breasts from the pigeons and skin them. Roughly chop the pigeon carcasses and reserve for the sauce. Dissolve the salt in the hot water in a large bowl, then stir in the cold water. Place the pigeon breasts in this brine and leave in the fridge for 12 hours. Drain and pat dry.

To make the sauce, heat the oil in a shallow frying pan. Add the carcasses and brown well; remove and set aside. Add the vegetables to the pan with the garlic and peppercorns and colour well. Deglaze with the wine, then reduce to a syrupy consistency. Return the carcasses to the pan and add the thyme and stock. Bring to a simmer and cook for 1 hour. Strain the sauce into a clean pan. Bring to the boil, skimming well, then season and set aside, ready to reheat for serving.

For the Yorkshire puddings, whisk the ingredients together in a bowl, then pass the batter through a fine sieve into a clean bowl or jug. Leave to rest in the fridge for 1 hour.

Preheat the oven to 200°C/400°F/gas mark 6. Put 1cm of oil in each hole of a 4-hole Yorkshire pudding tin that is 23cm square and 2cm deep. Heat in the oven for 10 minutes, then pour in the batter. Bake for 10 minutes, until risen and golden brown. When cooked, put a pudding on each plate.

Meanwhile, cook the pigeon breasts. Heat the oil in a pan, season the breasts and brown on both sides. Add the butter and cook, spooning the foaming butter over the breasts and turning them, for 4–10 minutes, until cooked to your liking. Remove and leave to rest for 5 minutes before slicing.

Fry the mushrooms and bacon in the oil until lightly browned. Add to the hot sauce with the pigeon breasts and parsley and serve inside the broken-open Yorkshire puddings.

· SOLES IN COFFINS ·

This macabre-sounding dish was originally made by curling sole in a scooped-out baked potato, topping with a vermouth sauce and brown shrimps and then baking. For our version here, we make a baked potato mash and pan-fry the sole. Tasty brown shrimps add a sweet saltiness to the dish, which is complemented by the aromatic vermouth sauce.

Serves 4

*2 large baking potatoes, scrubbed
and pricked
50g butter
50ml double cream
olive oil, for drizzling
4 lemon sole, filleted so the 2 fillets of each
fish are kept attached and then skinned
(ask your fishmonger to do this)
plain flour, for dusting
2 tbsp vegetable oil*

Sauce

*2 shallots, peeled and sliced
parsley and tarragon stalks
10g butter
5 black peppercorns
100ml dry vermouth
300ml fish stock
300ml double cream
juice of ½ lemon
100g peeled, cooked Morecambe Bay
brown shrimps
sea aster or chopped chervil
to garnish*

Preheat the oven to 180°C/350°F/gas mark 4. Bake the potatoes for about 1 hour, until cooked through. Cut in half and scrape out the flesh into a pan (reserve the skins). Mash with the butter and cream and season to taste. Set aside.

Cut each half potato skin into four strips, season and drizzle with olive oil. Spread out on a baking tray and set a second baking tray on top. Reduce the oven to 100°C/212°F/gas mark low and bake the skins for 1 hour, until crisp.

Meanwhile, make the sauce. Sweat the shallots with the parsley and tarragon stalks in the butter for 6–7 minutes, until well cooked. Add the peppercorns and vermouth and reduce by half. Add the fish stock and reduce by half, then add the cream and simmer gently until the desired consistency is reached. Season with the lemon juice and salt and pepper to taste.

Fold each sole fillet in three to form a pillow shape. Season and dust all over with flour. Heat the vegetable oil in a frying pan, add the sole and fry until golden brown on one side. Turn over and finish cooking. Meanwhile, heat the mashed potato and the vermouth sauce, stirring the brown shrimps into the hot sauce.

Serve the sole on the mash with the sauce spooned over. Garnish with strips of crisp potato skin and sea aster or chopped chervil.

· COCK-A-LEEKIE PIE ·

Heralded as Scotland's national soup, cock-a-leekie was originally a simple broth of chicken and leeks, garnished with prunes. The first recipe for the soup dates back to 1598. Instead of serving this as a soup we think it makes a great pie filling – it's warm and comforting and great for children.

Makes 1 large pie or 4 small pies

2 tbsp vegetable oil
400g skinless, boneless chicken breasts, cut into 2cm chunks
3 leeks, white part only, finely sliced
100g butter
100g plain flour
100ml white wine
150ml chicken stock
150ml milk
leaves from ¼ bunch of tarragon, chopped

300g good-quality puff pastry, thawed if frozen
2 free-range egg yolks, beaten

Preheat the oven to 180°C/350°F/gas mark 4. Heat the oil in a frying pan. Season the chicken pieces, then add to the pan and brown well. Remove to a bowl and set aside. Add the leeks and fry until softened. Season and add to the chicken.

Melt the butter in a saucepan. Stir in the flour and cook for 3 minutes. Gradually add the white wine, whisking continuously. Bring to a simmer and cook for 5 minutes, then add the stock and milk and gently simmer for a further 10 minutes, stirring well. Add the tarragon, then season with salt and pepper. Add to the chicken and leeks and stir to mix.

Roll out the pastry to a shape that will make a lid for your pie dish (or dishes): for a large pie use a 22cm diameter dish that is 4cm deep; or for small pies use four 11 x 5cm oval dishes that are 3.5cm deep. Cut a cross in the centre of the pastry lid.

Put a pie bird in the middle of the dish (this will allow steam to escape during baking so the underside of the pastry lid won't become soggy), then spoon in the chicken and leek filling around it. Brush the rim of the dish with beaten egg yolk, then lay the pastry lid over the top (the cross should fit over the pie bird) and press the edges to the rim of the dish to seal. Brush the pastry lid with beaten egg yolk. Bake for 20 minutes, until golden. Serve hot.

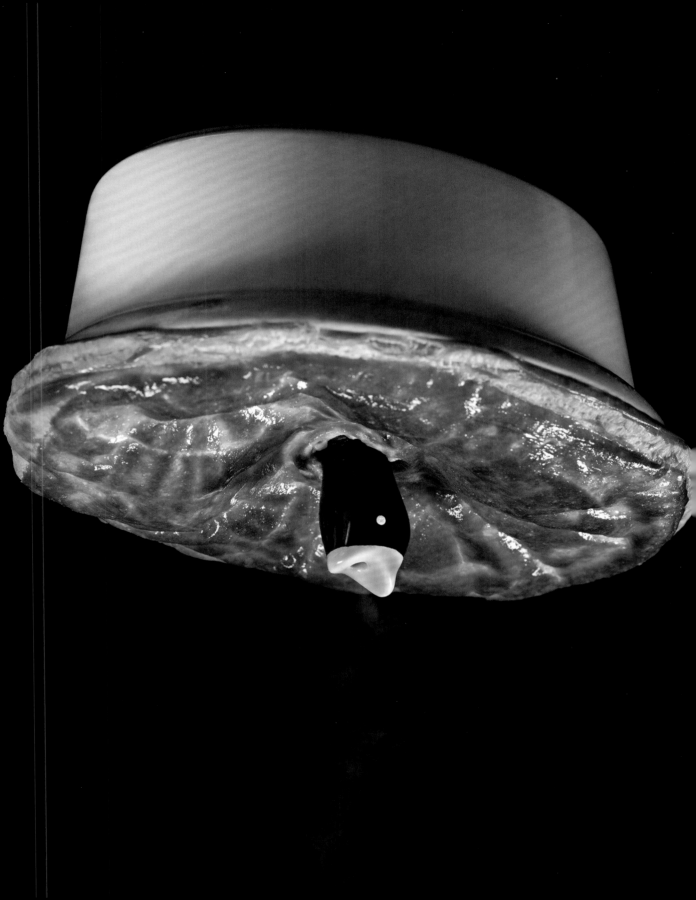

56

GLAMORGAN SAUSAGES

These were once the poor man's meatless substitute for the real thing and today make an interesting dish for vegetarians. Welsh by origin, they use Caerphilly cheese – a slightly tart yet robustly savoury, hard cheese.

Serves 4

175g fresh breadcrumbs
110g Caerphilly cheese, grated
1 small leek, very finely chopped
1 tbsp chopped parsley
pinch of English mustard powder
2 free-range eggs, 1 of them separated
4 tbsp milk
plain flour, for coating
1 tbsp vegetable oil
15g butter

Mix together the breadcrumbs, grated cheese, leek, parsley and mustard. Add 1 whole egg and 1 egg yolk and mix thoroughly. Add enough of the milk to bind the mixture together. Divide into eight portions and mould each into a sausage shape.

Beat the remaining egg white until frothy. Dip the sausages in the egg white, then roll in the flour to coat.

Heat the oil with the butter in a frying pan. Add the sausages and fry for 5–10 minutes, until golden brown all over. Serve hot or cold.

57

· TWEED KETTLE ·

Originating from around the river Tweed in Scotland, this dish originally involved stuffing a whole fish with herbs and nutmeg before baking. We played around with this and came up with the idea of a herb crust to bake on top of the fish. Served with a butter sauce, this is a comforting dish and quite simple to prepare.

Serves 4

4 square-cut portions of sea trout fillet, about 150g each, skinned

Crust
200g fresh white breadcrumbs (made without crusts)
100g soft butter
50g Parmesan cheese, finely grated
50g parsley, leaves chopped and stalks reserved
50g tarragon, leaves chopped and stalks reserved
50g dill, leaves chopped and stalks reserved
freshly grated nutmeg

Sauce
knob of butter
½ onion, peeled and finely chopped
¼ bunch of thyme
5 white peppercorns
100ml white wine
100ml fish or vegetable stock
50ml double cream
50g unsalted butter, diced
juice of ½ lemon

For the crust, put the breadcrumbs, soft butter, Parmesan, herb leaves, and nutmeg, salt and pepper to taste in a food processor. Blitz until thoroughly combined. Take a teaspoon of the mix and flatten it on a small baking tray, then grill to test: the crust mix should colour well without any butter splitting out. Roll out the crust mix between two sheets of greaseproof paper to a thickness of 5mm, and freeze. Once the crust is frozen, cut pieces to match the size of the trout portions.

While the crust is freezing, make the sauce. Heat a frying pan with the knob of butter. When foaming, add the onion with some seasoning and cook until soft. Add the thyme, reserved herb stalks and peppercorns and cook for a further 2 minutes. Add the white wine and reduce by half. Add the stock and reduce again by half. Strain through a fine sieve into a clean pan, then reduce to about 75ml. Add the cream and bring to a simmer. Reduce the heat and add the unsalted butter one cube at a time, whisking continuously. Season and add lemon juice to taste. Keep warm.

Preheat the oven to 180°C/350°F/gas mark 4. Place the fish on a greased baking tray and lay a piece of crust on each portion of fish. Bake for 5 minutes (the trout will be slightly pink in the centre). If the crust needs more colour, glaze under the grill for a few seconds. Serve with the butter sauce.

Fifteenth Years of the Reign of His present Majesty, for the Regulation and Improvement of the Fisheries in the River *Tweed*, and the Rivers and Streams running into the same, and also within the Mouth or Entrance of the said River. [3d *May* 1797.]

WHEREAS an Act was passed in the Eleventh Year of the Reign of His present Majesty, intituled, *An Act for regulating and improving the Fisheries in the River* Tweed, *and the Rivers and Streams running into the same, and also within the Mouth or Entrance of the said River*: And whereas also an Act was passed in the Fifteenth Year of the Reign of His present Majesty, for amending and rendering more effectual the said Act: And whereas, notwithstanding the Provisions of the said Acts, idle and disorderly Persons make a Practice of fishing for Salmon, Gilses, Salmon Trouts, and Whitlings, within the Mouth or Entrance of the said River *Tweed*, and by setting of Bob Nets and other Nets therein, intercept and obstruct the free Progress of such Fish into the said River, to the manifest Detriment and Loss of the Proprietors and Occupiers thereof: And whereas also, by Means of Sloops, Vessels, Cobles,

58

·HAM HOCK WITH CHAMP·
AND PARSLEY SAUCE

This is a real winter warmer. The thick, flavoursome parsley sauce is a take on the parsley liquor that is still served with pie, mash and jellied eels in the East End of London.

Serves 4

Ham hocks
2 smoked ham hocks
2 carrots, peeled and cut across in half
1 leek, white part only, cut across in half
6 white peppercorns
1 onion, peeled and halved
2 bay leaves
2 cloves garlic, peeled and lightly smashed

Parsley sauce
leaves from 1 large bunch of flat-leaf parsley

Champ
400g mashing potatoes, peeled and cut to the same size
50g butter
½ bunch of spring onions, finely sliced
100ml hot milk or cream
½ tsp salt

Begin by cooking the ham hocks. Put them in a large saucepan with the remaining ingredients and cover with water. Bring to the boil, then reduce to a simmer. Cook for 3–4 hours, until the bone can be pulled out of the meat. Lift out the hocks and set aside.

Strain the liquor through a fine sieve into a clean saucepan. Bring to the boil and reduce by a third (this makes a great jelly for pork pies etc.). Meanwhile, gently break up the meat from the ham hocks, discarding any sinew amd keeping the pieces as chunky as possible; cover and keep hot. (You can prepare this ahead of time. Before serving, put the pieces of ham hock in an ovenproof dish with a little of the cooking liquor to moisten, cover with foil and reheat in a preheated 180°C/350°F/gas mark 4 oven for 15 minutes.)

For the parsley sauce, bring a saucepan of salted water to the boil, add the parsley and blanch for 30 seconds. Drain and refresh under cold running water, then repeat the blanching. Drain and place in a blender. Blitz with enough of the ham hock cooking liquor to make a smooth sauce. Pour into a small saucepan, ready to heat through before serving.

For the champ, put the potatoes in a pan of salted water and bring to the boil. Cook until tender, then drain well and mash. Melt the butter in a frying pan, add the spring onions and cook lightly for 2 minutes. Add the butter and onions to the mash along with the hot milk or cream and salt. Mash together until smooth.

Serve the ham hock with the parsley sauce and champ.

· THE QUEEN'S POTAGE ·

A dish based on a recipe in John Nott's cookery book of 1723, this focuses more on the chicken than the broth. Traditionally for a potage, meat and vegetables were boiled together with water until they became very soft and formed a thick mush. Not too desirable in today's world! Pomegranate seeds and pistachios were used to garnish, to represent jewels and the wealth of the Royals.

Serves 4

4 skinless, boneless free-range chicken breasts
3 tbsp vegetable oil
¼ bunch of thyme
2 bay leaves
50g butter
200g mixed mushrooms, sliced
4 tbsp pomegranate seeds
2 tbsp toasted pistachio nuts (unsalted)

Broth

2 tbsp vegetable oil
200g button mushrooms, sliced
1 onion, peeled and sliced
1 bulb garlic, quartered
50ml white wine
3 sprigs of thyme
¼ bunch of tarragon
500ml chicken stock

Coating

50g butter
200g brioche, made into crumbs
1 tbsp thyme leaves
½ tsp salt
freshly ground black pepper to taste

Begin by making the broth. Heat the vegetable oil in a saucepan and fry the mushrooms, in batches, until nicely browned. Set aside. Add the onion and garlic to the pan and cook until soft and golden. Deglaze with the white wine and cook until reduced to a syrup. Add the herbs and stock and return the mushrooms to the pan. Bring to a boil, then simmer for 30 minutes. Pass through a fine sieve into a clean pan and set aside.

For the coating, melt the butter and mix with the crumbs, thyme and seasoning. Pat on to the chicken breasts to coat all over. Refrigerate until firm.

Preheat the oven to 180°C/350°F/gas mark 4. Heat 2 tablespoons of the oil in an ovenproof frying pan. Add the chicken and brown lightly. Add the herbs to the pan with the butter. When the butter is foaming, spoon it over the chicken and continue cooking for 5 minutes. Transfer the pan to the oven and bake for 6–8 minutes, until the breasts are almost cooked through. Remove from the oven and allow to rest for 5 minutes.

Fry the mushrooms in the remaining oil until golden and the liquid they exude has evaporated. Bring the broth back to the boil and adjust the seasoning if necessary.

Place the chicken breasts in shallow serving bowls, spoon over the hot broth and garnish with the pomegranate seeds, pistachios and mushrooms.

DORSET JUGGED STEAK
WITH CLAPSHOT

Traditionally, jugged dishes have blood in them to thicken the
sauce. The version here leaves out the blood while still creating an
unctuous gravy. Potato and turnip clapshot and pork meatballs are
great with the braised steak, making a really satisfying meal.
This is always our most popular dish in winter.

Serves 4

2 tbsp vegetable oil
4 x 200g featherblade steaks
1 onion, peeled and halved
4 cloves garlic, peeled and lightly smashed
2 carrots, peeled and cut across in half
1 leek, white part only, cut across in half
¼ bunch of thyme
¼ bunch of tarragon
2 bay leaves
4 star anise
5 white peppercorns
2 tbsp tomato purée
250ml red wine
1 litre beef stock
4 tbsp redcurrant jelly

Meatballs

200g pork sausage meat
1 tbsp chopped sage
½ tsp salt
2 tbsp chopped dried cranberries
1 tbsp vegetable oil, for frying

Clapshot

200g turnips, peeled and diced
200g mashing potatoes, peeled and diced
½ tsp salt · 25g butter · 100ml milk
1 tbsp chopped chives (optional)

Heat the oil in a large, wide saucepan or flameproof casserole
over a moderate heat. Season the featherblade steaks, then
brown all over. Remove from the pan. Add the onion, garlic,
carrots, leek, herbs and spices and fry until the vegetables are
lightly caramelized. Add the tomato purée and wine and
reduce to a syrup. Add the stock and bring to the boil.
Return the steaks to the pan, then cover and simmer gently
for 1 hour, until very tender.

Meanwhile, make the meatballs. Thoroughly mix together
the sausage meat, sage, salt and cranberries, then shape into
12 meatballs. Fry in the hot oil in a frying pan until evenly
browned and cooked through. When the meatballs are ready,
remove from the pan and keep them hot.

While the meatballs are cooking, make the clapshot. Put the
turnips and potatoes into a pan of salted water and bring
to the boil. Cook until tender, then drain well and mash
together with salt, butter and milk. Add the chives, if you
like. Keep hot.

Carefully remove the steaks from the pan; cover and keep
hot. Strain the sauce into a clean pan and bring back to a
gentle simmer, then reduce by a third. Stir in the redcurrant
jelly and check the seasoning, adding more salt if necessary.

To serve, pour the sauce over the steaks. Top with the
meatballs and serve the clapshot on the side.

61

· GROUSE ·
(AKIN TO MRS BEETON'S RECIPE)

The 'Glorious Twelfth' refers to the day that the grouse shooting season begins – the 12th of August. Game enthusiasts look forward to this, and it signifies the time that we add game to our menu. We wait until at least 5 days after the first day of shooting to ensure that the birds have been well hung, and thus are full of their unique earthy, rich flavour.

Serves 4

2 tbsp vegetable oil
4 grouse (from a reputable butcher), well hung
50g butter
¼ bunch of thyme
2 bay leaves
3 cloves garlic, peeled and lightly smashed
100ml red wine
1 tbsp red wine vinegar or sherry vinegar
200ml chicken stock
2 tbsp redcurrant jelly
8 rashers streaky bacon, cooked until crisp

Chicken liver pâté
1 tbsp vegetable oil
100g chicken livers
½ tsp salt
½ onion, peeled and sliced
1 clove garlic, peeled and finely diced
2 tbsp brandy
2 tbsp port
50g butter, melted

4 slices of brioche, toasted just before serving

Begin with the pâté. Set a large frying pan on a high heat and add a little of the oil. When almost smoking, season the livers with the salt and place them in the pan. Sear until browned all over. Transfer to a blender. Add the rest of the oil to the pan, then add the onion and garlic and cook until lightly golden. Add the brandy and port and cook, stirring, until the liquid has almost all evaporated. Transfer to the blender. Blitz the liver mixture until smooth. With the motor running, drizzle in the butter. Pass the mixture through a fine sieve into a bowl. Adjust the seasoning with more salt, if necessary, then leave to set in the fridge for 2 hours.

To cook the grouse, preheat the oven to 180°C/350°F/gas mark 4. Heat an ovenproof frying pan with the vegetable oil until hot. Season the grouse all over, then brown in the hot oil. Add the butter, herbs and garlic to the pan. When the butter foams, start spooning it over the grouse. Continue cooking, spooning over the butter, for 5 minutes, then place the pan in the oven to finish cooking for 10 minutes. Remove from the oven and lift the grouse on to a board. Leave to rest in a warm place for 10 minutes while you finish the sauce.

Heat the fat remaining in the pan until foaming, then deglaze with the red wine and vinegar. Allow to simmer until the liquid has reduced by half, then add the stock and again reduce by half. Add the redcurrant jelly and season to taste. Strain through a fine sieve and keep hot.

Carve the grouse, cutting down either side of the breast bone, and place the crisp bacon rashers inside. Set a large quenelle of pâté on each slice of toasted brioche and serve with the grouse and the sauce.

KITCHEN TABLE

Our Kitchen Table is a wonderful arc-shaped table located right at the front of our kitchen. We offer five- or eight-course tasting menus here, where diners can share a meal while being able to see how it is prepared, and meeting the cooks who have created it.

The recipes in this chapter are all for sharing boards. We do various versions of these depending on the day of the week (for example, a roast on Sunday) and the seasons. I have selected a few of my favourites for you to try for yourself. It is, of course, very important with all of these to start off with the best quality meat, otherwise the result will not be as good as it could be.

In today's fast-paced world, many people seem to have lost the habit of buying their meat from a butcher's shop. We are very lucky at the restaurant being able to source some fantastic meat from the Lake District and elsewhere in the United Kingdom. I urge you to look further afield than the supermarket, and visit butcher's shops and farm stores where you can get more unusual cuts as well as lots of useful information.

BEEF: RIBEYE, TONGUE, BONE MARROW, CALF'S LIVER

We source our ribeyes from Lake District Farmers. Their beef is succulent, tender and full of flavour. We cook, and serve, the ribs with the bone on as we feel it adds even more flavour to the dish. On the board with the ribeye we serve beef in other guises – thin slices of pressed ox tongue, calf's liver sautéed in butter, and rich, savoury bone marrow. The latter is an ingredient that has become a lot more 'in vogue' in the past year or two, which I'm glad about as it is such a unique ingredient.

Serves 2

Ox tongue

1 small ox tongue
4 bay leaves
100ml white wine vinegar
1 onion, peeled and quartered
2 cloves garlic, peeled and left whole
1 carrot, peeled and cut across in half
1 leek, white part only, cut across in half
6 white peppercorns
1 tsp coriander seeds
¼ bunch of thyme

Ribeye

1 x 500g ribeye steak on the bone, about 4cm thick
50ml pomace oil
2 sprigs thyme
2 sprigs rosemary
1 bay leaf
1 clove garlic, peeled and crushed
25g unsalted butter

Scrub the tongue well with a stiff brush under running cold water, then place in a bowl of cold water to soak for at least 6 hours. Drain the tongue, transfer to a deep saucepan and cover with fresh cold water. Set on a moderate heat and bring to the boil, skimming off any scum that appears. Add all of the remaining ingredients for the tongue and simmer very gently for 3–3½ hours, until the bone at the end of the tongue can be pulled away easily.

Remove the tongue from the cooking liquor and peel off the skin. Trim off the gristle and root, then place the tongue in a dish. Cover with clingfilm and set aside. Strain the cooking liquor through a fine sieve into a clean saucepan and reduce by a third. Cool, then pour around the tongue. Cover the tongue with a plate and weigh down with tins of food. Place in the fridge to press for 3 hours. (This will make more than two servings, but the remainder can be kept in the fridge for up to 5 days.)

Place the steak in a plastic bag. Add the oil, herbs and garlic. Remove as much air from the bag as you can, then tightly wrap it in clingfilm. Leave to marinate in the fridge for at least 3 hours (or up to 72 hours).

continued overleaf

Red wine sauce
2 tbsp vegetable oil
80g beef trimmings or rump steak, diced
1 onion, peeled and diced
1 carrot, peeled and diced
1 stick celery, diced
2 cloves garlic, peeled and left whole
2 tbsp tomato purée
1 bay leaf
4 black peppercorns
250ml red wine
300ml beef or chicken stock
½ tsp salt
¼ bunch of tarragon

Bone marrow
1 tbsp vegetable oil
4 pieces bone marrow

Calf's liver
1 tbsp vegetable oil
100g calf's liver, cut into 3cm slices
a large knob of butter

To serve
olive oil
fresh horseradish
2 rashers bacon, fried until crisp
watercress

For the red wine sauce, heat a saucepan over a high heat with half of the vegetable oil. Season the beef, then add to the pan and fry until dark golden. Remove and set aside. Add the onion, carrot, celery and garlic to the pan with the remaining oil and brown the vegetables. Add the tomato purée, bay leaf, peppercorns and red wine. Bring to the boil, then simmer gently until syrupy. Add the remaining ingredients and the browned beef. Simmer for 30 minutes, skimming regularly to remove any fat. Strain into a clean pan, then adjust the seasoning if necessary. Set aside, ready to reheat for serving.

To cook the ribeye, preheat the oven to 180°C/350°F/gas mark 4. Heat a large, ovenproof frying pan with the oil from the marinade until almost smoking. Season the ribeye with salt, then brown on both sides in the pan. Add the unsalted butter as well as the herbs from the marinade. When the butter begins to foam, spoon it over the meat to baste. Transfer the pan to the oven and cook for 5 minutes. Turn the steak over, then return to the oven and cook for another 5 minutes. Remove the ribeye from the pan and leave somewhere warm to rest for at least 15 minutes.

For the bone marrow, heat the oil in a pan, season the marrow and brown well on each side. Leave the marrow to cook through for 5 minutes.

Meanwhile, for the liver, heat the oil in another pan until almost smoking, season the liver and quickly brown on each side. Add the butter and finish cooking.

Slice the tongue very thinly (about 3mm), rub with olive oil and season with salt and pepper.

Slice the ribeye and arrange on a warmed board (reheat it for 5 minutes in the turned-off oven, if necessary). Grate some fresh horseradish on to the board, then add the ribeye bone, liver, bone marrow, bacon, sliced tongue and watercress. Serve with the hot red wine sauce.

·CHICKEN: BREAST, SAUSAGE· ROLLS, CRISPY SKIN, BARBECUE WINGS

This combines all of the best elements of chicken in one sharing board – tender breast, wings with a sticky glaze and juicy leg meat wrapped in pastry to create a chicken sausage roll. And there's the crispy chicken skin too. Buy free-range, corn-fed chickens if possible, because they have a richer flavour and texture.

Serves 4

Barbecue chicken wings
50g tomato purée
1 tbsp black treacle
1 tbsp Worcestershire sauce
½ tsp sweet smoked paprika
½ tsp hot smoked paprika
juice of ½ lemon
1 clove garlic, peeled and finely chopped
8 chicken wings

Chicken breast
2 boneless free-range chicken breasts, skinned (reserve the skin for the crispy skin)
1 tsp salt
50ml hot water
450ml cold water
1 tbsp vegetable oil
large knob of butter
4 sprigs thyme
150ml chicken stock

Start with the barbecue chicken wings. Mix together all of the ingredients for the barbecue sauce, adding a good pinch of salt. Pour half of the sauce into a second bowl, add the chicken wings and marinate for at least 4 hours, or overnight, in the fridge. Set the remaining sauce aside.

The next day, brine the chicken breasts. Dissolve the salt in the hot water in a bowl, then add the cold water. Submerge the chicken breasts in this brine and leave for 1½ hours. Drain and pat dry.

While the chicken breasts are in the brine, make the sausage rolls. Mince the chicken leg meat using a mincer or a food processor. Transfer to a bowl and add all the remaining ingredients except the pastry, egg yolks and sea salt. Mix well together.

Divide the puff pastry in half. Roll out one piece on a lightly floured surface to a rectangle 3mm thick. Spoon on half of the chicken mix and spread evenly over three-quarters of the pastry sheet. Brush the remaining quarter of the pastry sheet with egg yolk, then roll the pastry over the filling and continue to roll up to form a cylinder. Repeat with the remaining pastry sheet and chicken mix. Place the cylinders in the freezer for 10 minutes to firm up.

continued overleaf

Chicken sausage rolls

300g chicken leg meat (reserve the
skin from the chicken legs
for the crispy skin)
leaves from ¼ bunch of thyme
¼ bunch of parsley, chopped
¼ bunch of sage, chopped
1 medium onion, peeled and diced
1 tbsp soy sauce
½ tsp freshly grated nutmeg
¼ tsp curry powder
100g mixed mushrooms, sautéed in
a knob of butter, seasoned
well and chopped
50ml cream (single or double)
½ tsp salt
freshly ground black pepper to taste
320g all-butter puff pastry
(thawed if frozen)
2 free-range egg yolks, beaten
Maldon sea salt

Brush the cylinders with egg yolk and sprinkle with sea salt. Using a very sharp knife, carefully cut each cylinder across in half. Arrange on a baking tray lined with baking parchment and set aside in a cool place.

For the crispy skin, remove any excess fat from the skin of the chicken breasts and legs, then spread out on a baking tray lined with baking parchment. Season well. Set another sheet of baking parchment on top and then another baking tray, to keep the skin flat. Set aside.

When ready to cook, preheat the oven to 200°C/400°F/gas mark 6. Transfer the chicken wings to a baking tray and smother with the rest of the barbecue sauce. Bake for about 20 minutes, until crisp and cooked through. Remove from the oven and keep warm. Reduce the oven temperature to 180°C/350°F/gas mark 4. (If you have two ovens, you can cook the wings in one and the chicken breasts, skin and sausage rolls in the other, simultaneously.)

For the chicken breasts, heat an ovenproof frying pan with the vegetable oil and brown the breasts all over. Add the butter with the thyme and, when foaming, spoon the butter over the chicken for a few minutes. Add the stock and bring to the boil, then cover the pan with foil and transfer to the oven. Bake for 10–15 minutes, until the breasts are cooked through.

At the same time, bake the chicken skin for 10–15 minutes, until golden and crispy. Also bake the chicken sausage rolls for 15–20 minutes, until risen and golden.

To serve, carve the chicken breasts and arrange with everything else on a sharing board.

LAMB: FILLET, SLOW-COOKED SHOULDER, LAMB BURGERS

Lamb loin fillets are lean, tender and quick to fry, contrasting well with soft, succulent lamb shoulder that has been gently cooked for hours. The mini lamb burgers add a touch of fun to the board – they're often the first things to go when we put them down on the Kitchen Table.

Serves 6–8

Slow-cooked lamb shoulder
2 onions, peeled and quartered
2 bulbs garlic, broken into cloves
but not peeled
1 large bunch of rosemary
¼ bunch of thyme
1 x 1.5–2kg good-quality lamb
shoulder on the bone
2 tbsp olive oil
1 tbsp salt
freshly ground black pepper to taste
150ml white wine
500ml chicken or vegetable stock

Lamb fillet
4 lamb loin fillets, about 450g in total
(ask your butcher for these)
50ml pomace oil
1 stalk rosemary
2 sprigs thyme
1 clove garlic, peeled and lightly crushed

Start the shoulder first. Preheat the oven to 200°C/400°F/gas mark 6. Put the onions, garlic, rosemary and thyme in the bottom of a roasting tray. Score the fat of the shoulder with a sharp knife, making diagonal lines one way and then the other, to create a criss-cross pattern. Set in the tray on top of the flavourings. Rub the shoulder with the olive oil, then sprinkle with the salt and some pepper. Cover the tray with foil and place in the oven, immediately turning down the temperature to 160°C/325°F/gas mark 3. Cook for 3 hours, then remove the foil and continue cooking for 45 minutes.

While the shoulder is in the oven, place the lamb fillets in a shallow dish with the oil, herbs and garlic. Cover and leave to marinate in a cool place for 2 hours.

Mix together all of the ingredients for the burgers with some pepper. Fry a little of the mix to check the seasoning; adjust if necessary. Shape into four small patties, or two larger ones if you prefer. Keep in a cool place until ready to cook.

Remove the lamb shoulder from the tray to a semi-deep dish; cover with foil and set aside in a warm place. Pour the onion mix and cooking juices into a saucepan set over a medium heat. When hot, add the wine and cook until reduced to a syrup. Add the stock and simmer for 25 minutes, skimming about half the fat off the top (or more if you prefer, although lamb fat has incredible flavour). Check the seasoning and adjust if necessary, then pass the sauce through a fine sieve into a clean pan. Set aside.

Lamb burgers

300g lean lamb mince
2 tbsp chopped flat-leaf parsley leaves
1 tsp thyme leaves
¼ onion, peeled and finely diced
1 clove garlic, peeled and finely crushed
1 tbsp Worcestershire sauce
1 tbsp tomato purée
1 free-range egg, beaten
½ tsp salt
vegetable oil, for frying

To serve

4 mini burger buns or 2 large buns, split open
2 tbsp home-made or good-quality purchased mayonnaise
1 tsp chopped mint leaves
1 tsp mint sauce
4 drops chipotle Tabasco sauce

Now cook the burgers. Heat a frying pan with 1 tablespoon oil, then fry the patties for about 10 minutes, until they are well browned on both sides and cooked through. Meanwhile, lightly toast the buns, and mix the mayonnaise with the mint, mint sauce and Tabasco.

When the burgers are nearly ready, heat a frying pan with some of the oily marinade from the lamb fillets. When hot, season the fillets well and flash fry quickly on all sides to brown well. Remove from the pan and leave to rest for a few minutes. Reheat the sauce for the lamb shoulder.

Place the lamb burgers in the buns, topping the burgers with the mayonnaise.

To serve, ensure everything is hot (you may need to reheat the shoulder in the oven for 5–10 minutes). Carve each loin into two; carve the shoulder; and cut small burgers in half and large burgers into quarters. Arrange everything on a warm carving board and serve with the sauce.

PORK: SLOW-COOKED BELLY, HONEY-GLAZED BACON, SAUSAGES, CRACKLING

Pork belly has to be one of my favourite cuts of meat. When it is cooked slowly, to allow the fat to render down, the result is super moist and succulent. Baking the belly on top of apples adds another dimension, enhancing the sweetness of the meat while creating the basis for an apple sauce to serve alongside. Fantastic honey-glazed bacon and herby sausages are on the board too, and no roast pork dish is complete without the crackling.

Serves 6–8

Slow-cooked belly
1 x 400g piece pork belly
rock salt
4 Granny Smith apples
1 onion, peeled and sliced
¼ bunch of thyme

Home-made sausages
1 onion, peeled and finely diced
1 clove garlic, peeled and crushed
leaves from ¼ bunch of thyme
25g butter
300g pork mince
100g pork sausage meat
1 tbsp grain mustard
leaves from ¼ bunch of sage, chopped
¼ bunch of parsley, chopped
½ tsp ground mace
½ tsp salt
freshly ground black pepper to taste
vegetable oil, for frying
8 sausage casings (optional)

Rub the pork belly all over with rock salt, then cover and leave in a cool place overnight. The next day, rinse off the salt with cold water and pat the pork dry. Set aside.

To make the sausages, sauté the onion with the garlic and thyme in the butter until soft. Transfer to a bowl and add the pork mince, sausage meat, mustard, sage, parsley, mace, salt and some pepper. Mix well together. Fry a little of the mix to check the seasoning; adjust as necessary.

Pipe into the sausage casings. Alternatively, lay out a sheet of clingfilm on the work surface and place one-quarter of the mixture along the edge of it in a line 15cm long. Roll the clingfilm over the mix and continue rolling tightly to form a sausage shape, tying each end tightly. Twist in the middle to make two sausages. Repeat with the remaining mix. Bring a large saucepan of water to the boil, add the sausages (in casings or clingfilm) and simmer for about 3 minutes. Drain and allow to cool, then keep in the fridge until needed.

Next cook the pork belly. Preheat your oven to 150°C/300°F/gas mark 2. Quarter and core the apples, then place in a roasting dish just large enough to fit the pork belly. Add the onion and thyme. Set the pork belly on top. Cover with foil and cook in the oven for 3 hours.

Honey-glazed bacon
4 tbsp honey
1 tsp grain mustard
2 tbsp soy sauce
1 star anise, grated
½ tsp freshly grated nutmeg
*1 x 200g boneless unsmoked bacon joint
(ideally 5cm thick)*

½ apple, sliced, to garnish

Remove from the oven and lift off the skin; reserve this. Transfer the pork to a carving board, cover with foil and set aside in a warm place.

Increase the heat of the oven to 180°C/350°F/gas mark 4. Place the pork skin on a baking tray and bake for about 10 minutes, until crisp. Slice the crackling into pieces. Set aside with the pork belly.

For the apple sauce, remove the thyme and any large areas of fat from the roasting dish, then transfer the apples and onion with the cooking liquor to a blender and blend until smooth. Adjust the seasoning and pass through a sieve into a saucepan. Set aside; reheat for serving.

To cook the bacon, mix together the honey, mustard, soy sauce, star anise and nutmeg and brush half of this liberally over all sides of the bacon. Set it in a small roasting dish, cover with foil and place in the oven to cook for about 10 minutes. Remove the foil, brush with the remaining honey mix and bake for a further 5 minutes.

Meanwhile, cook the sausages. Remove the clingfilm if you used it, and fry the sausages in a little oil for about 5 minutes, until golden all over and cooked through.

To serve, ensure everything is hot (if not, reheat in the oven for 5–10 minutes). Set the pork belly on a warmed board and carve into eight slices. Slice the bacon too. Add the sausages and crackling. Garnish the board with a stack of apple slices and serve with the apple sauce.

PORK: SLOW-COOKED BELLY,
HONEY-GLAZED BACON,
SAUSAGES, CRACKLING

VENISON: BRAISED HAUNCH, FAGGOTS, CROQUETTES

Haunch of venison is packed full of flavour and when braised it really is the perfect winter comfort food. Here the lean meat is served with caul-wrapped venison and bacon faggots, crisp venison croquettes spiked with port-soaked cranberries, and a rich cauliflower side dish.

Serves 8

Braised haunch of venison
1 x 1kg boned haunch of venison
2 tbsp vegetable oil
1 carrot, peeled and cut across into quarters
1 leek, white part only, cut across into quarters
1 stick celery, cut across in half
1 onion, peeled and halved
2 bay leaves
10 juniper berries
2 cloves
2 cinnamon sticks
200ml red wine
200ml port
50ml red wine vinegar
2 tbsp treacle
1 litre chicken stock
1 litre veal or beef stock

Venison faggots
100g venison or pork liver
200g boneless venison meat
100g pork belly, cut into chunks
100g smoked back bacon, diced
1 onion, peeled and diced
2 garlic cloves, peeled and crushed

Preheat the oven to 100°C/215°F/gas mark low. Season the haunch. Heat a large flameproof casserole with the oil and brown the haunch evenly on all sides. Remove and set aside. Add the vegetables to the casserole with the bay leaves and spices, and lightly brown. Pour in the wine, port and vinegar and reduce by a third, then add the treacle and stocks and bring to the boil. Place the haunch in the liquid and cover the casserole with foil. Transfer to the oven to braise for 8 hours.

Remove the casserole from the oven. Lift out the haunch and wrap in foil; set aside. Pass the cooking liquor through a sieve into a clean pan and bring to the boil, then reduce by a third. Adjust the seasoning, if necessary. Break the venison down to large chunks and place in the sauce. Cool, then cover and keep in the fridge until needed.

Next make the faggots. Remove any sinew from the liver and venison, then cut into chunks. Mince together with the pork belly, bacon, onion and garlic using a mincer or food processor (take care not to purée). Mix in the remaining ingredients. Fry a small portion to check the seasoning; adjust if necessary. Divide the mix into eight portions and roll each into a ball. Wrap in caul fat and set aside in a cool place.

For the croquettes, bring the port to the boil in a small pan and add the cranberries; cover and set aside to soak. Heat the oil in a frying pan and add the onion, seasoning well. Cook until softened, then add the butter and continue to cook until golden and sweet.

100g fresh breadcrumbs
leaves from ¼ bunch of flat-leaf
parsley, chopped
leaves from ¼ bunch of thyme
25ml port
1 tsp freshly grated nutmeg
3 juniper berries, crushed
grated zest of ½ orange
1 tsp salt
caul fat, for wrapping
vegetable oil, for frying

Venison and cranberry croquettes
50ml port
50g dried cranberries, chopped
1 tbsp vegetable oil
1 onion, peeled and sliced
large knob of butter
250g cooked venison (from
haunch of venison)
leaves from ¼ bunch of thyme
100g button mushrooms, diced
and browned in butter
100ml venison sauce (from haunch
of venison), warmed
vegetable oil, for deep-frying
2 free-range eggs
100g panko breadcrumbs
50g plain flour

Cauliflower pudding
1 small cauliflower, about 180g,
broken into florets
500ml milk
½ onion, peeled
4 cloves
50g unsalted butter
50g plain flour
50g Cheddar cheese, grated, plus
extra for sprinkling
½ tsp freshly grated nutmeg

Break the venison into small chunks and combine in a bowl with the onion, thyme, cranberries, mushrooms and sauce. Season well with salt and pepper. Press into a 3cm-thick layer in a deep dish lined with a double layer of clingfilm. Cover the dish tightly with clingfilm and place in the fridge to firm up for at least 3 hours.

Meanwhile, prepare the cauliflower pudding. Add the cauliflower florets to a pan of boiling water and blanch for about 3 minutes. Drain and refresh in iced water, then drain again and set aside. Put the milk in a saucepan with the onion studded with the cloves, bring to a simmer and cook for 5 minutes. Cover and set aside to infuse for 30 minutes.

Melt the butter in a saucepan, add the flour and cook for a few minutes, stirring. Pour in a little of the infused milk, whisking well, then add the remaining milk (discard the clove-studded onion). Cook over a moderate heat, stirring, until the sauce is thick and the floury taste has cooked out. Add the cheese and mix well, then season with the nutmeg, salt and pepper. Fold in the cauliflower. Transfer to a baking dish and sprinkle with extra grated cheese.

When ready to serve, preheat the oven to 180°C/350°F/ gas mark 4.

Heat some oil in an ovenproof frying pan and brown the faggots all over. Add 50ml of the sauce from the venison haunch and cover the pan with foil. Transfer to the oven to cook for about 20 minutes. Place the braised haunch and its sauce in a baking dish, cover and reheat in the oven for about 10 minutes. At the same time, place the cauliflower pudding in the oven to cook for 10 minutes. (If you like, finish off under a hot grill to brown the cheese.)

Meanwhile, fry the croquettes. Heat oil for deep-frying to 170°C. Lightly beat the eggs in a shallow bowl and put the panko crumbs and flour on two plates. Cut the croquette mix into squares. Dust each one with flour, shaking off the excess, then dip in beaten egg and finally coat in crumbs. Fry, in batches, for about 6 minutes, until golden all over and hot in the centre. Drain on kitchen paper.

To serve, arrange everything on a sharing board.

VENISON: BRAISED HAUNCH, FAGGOTS, CROQUETTES

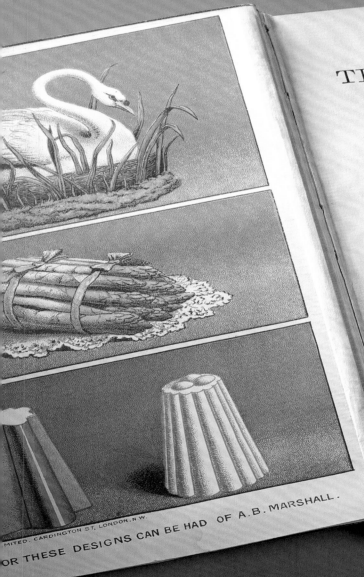

MITED, CARDINGTON ST, LONDON, N.W.

...OR THESE DESIGNS CAN BE HAD OF A.B. MARSHALL.

TENTH THOUSAND.

THE BOOK OF ICES.

INCLUDING

CREAM AND WATER ICES,
SORBETS, MOUSSES, ICED SOUFFLÉS, AND
VARIOUS ICED DISHES,

WITH

NAMES IN FRENCH AND ENGLISH,

AND

VARIOUS COLOURED DESIGNS FOR ICES.

BY

A. B. MARSHALL.

(Copyright.)

London:

MARSHALL'S SCHOOL OF COOKERY, 30 & 32,

AND

SIMPKIN, MARSHALL, HAMILTON, KEN

4, STATIONERS'-HALL COU

ESTABLISHED 1857.

[*Price Half-a-Crown*

PUDDINGS

As the old proverb states, the proof of the pudding is in the eating. I could not agree more. Puddings are very much a subjective thing, dependent on how sweet your tooth is as well as the mood you're in. And, of course, your pudding appetite will also depend on what you have already eaten, although most people seem to find a little room left for something sweet. I love puddings, especially chocolate puddings (the warm chocolate in a pot in this chapter is one of my favourites).

To be a serious pudding cook, you need to have a few essential items in your kitchen. For me, these are a must: a substantial free-standing electric mixer, a rubber spatula, a large and a small whisk, and an accurate set of scales.

· PEANUT BUTTER ICE CREAM ·

This has to be one of my favourite ice creams of all time, so even though it isn't traditionally British, I couldn't resist including it in this book. At the restaurant, we use this to make a choc ice because peanut and chocolate is such a good combination.

Serves 6

300ml whole milk
200g smooth peanut butter
4 free-range eggs, separated
150g caster sugar
400ml whipping cream

Peanut brittle
50g caster sugar
pinch of salt
50g roasted peanuts

First make the peanut brittle. Put the sugar into a saucepan set over a high heat. When the sugar begins to melt, swirl the pan to move it around. When it turns to a dark caramel, add the salt and peanuts and mix well with a spatula. Turn out on to a silicone mat or heatproof surface and smooth out, then allow to cool. When cool and set, roughly chop the brittle.

For the ice cream base, put the milk and peanut butter in a heavy-based saucepan and bring to the boil, then remove from the heat. Whisk the egg yolks with 50g of the sugar in a bowl. Whisk in a little of the hot milk, then add this mix to the rest of the hot milk in the saucepan. Cook over a low heat, stirring constantly with a wooden spoon, until the custard is thick enough to coat the back of the spoon. Add 100ml of the cream, then pour through a fine sieve into a shallow container. Cover the surface of the custard with clingfilm to prevent a skin from forming, then cool and chill.

Whip the remaining 300ml cream to soft peaks and set aside. Whisk the egg whites until stiff peaks form, then add the remaining 100g sugar and whisk until smooth and glossy.

Fold the custard and whipped cream together. Mix in the peanut brittle. Fold in a quarter of the egg whites, then add the remaining whites and mix gently. Transfer the mixture to a freezer container and cover with a lid. Freeze for 2–4 hours, until firm enough to scoop.

The ice cream can be kept in the freezer for 4–5 days. About 20 minutes before serving, transfer it to the fridge so it can soften a bit.

·BANANA STICKY TOFFEE· PUDDING

The origins of the classic British sticky toffee pudding seem to be rather contested, with the favourite story being that it was created by Samuel Coulson's cook in the Lake District in 1960. The addition of banana adds another layer of sweetness and density that complements the pudding very well.

Makes 8 puddings

Banana caramel sauce
75g caster sugar
50g golden syrup
50ml crème de banane (banana liqueur)
1 overripe banana, sliced
120ml whipping cream, heated
½ tsp salt
25g unsalted butter

Cake
100g soft unsalted butter
100g caster sugar
2 free-range eggs
2 overripe bananas, mashed
4g bicarbonate of soda
50ml hot milk
4g baking powder
160g plain flour

Begin by making the caramel sauce. Put the sugar and golden syrup into a saucepan over a high heat and allow the mix to caramelize until it is a very dark brown; do not stir but instead swirl the pan to move the mix about. Very carefully add the liqueur (the mix will spit) followed by the banana and cream, then whisk together, adding the salt. When smoothly combined, remove from the heat and whisk in the butter. Set aside.

Preheat the oven to 180°C/350°F/gas mark 4. To make the cake mixture, cream the butter and sugar together in a large bowl. Add the eggs and bananas, mixing well. Stir the bicarbonate of soda into the milk, then add to the bowl and mix. Sift the baking powder and flour together, then fold into the cake mix until just combined.

Grease eight of the cups in a 12-hole muffin tin. Add a large spoonful of caramel sauce to each greased cup (keep the rest of the sauce for serving), then divide the cake mixture among the cups. Bake for 20–25 minutes, until risen and golden. Turn out, spoon over the remaining caramel sauce and serve hot.

Alternatively, for an even saucier treat, leave to cool, then turn out and cut a cone shape out of the bottom of each cake. Fill with more caramel sauce, then place the cone back inside the cake and set it back in the muffin tin. When ready to serve, reheat in a preheated 180°C/350°F/gas mark 4 oven for 10 minutes.

· ETON MESS ·

Some say this pudding came about because a batch of meringues was crushed on the way to a picnic at Eton, and fruit was added to the 'mess', but the College maintains that the dish was originally made there just with fruit and cream or ice cream, with meringue being a later addition. In the restaurant, rather than serving the pudding in the traditional way, we leave our guests to make their own messes and serve a perfect meringue filled with the luscious raspberry cream.

Serves 6

350g raspberries
200ml double cream
2 tbsp raspberry jam
25ml crème de framboise (raspberry liqueur – optional)

Meringues
80g (about 3) free-range egg whites
80g caster sugar
80g icing sugar
2 tbsp freeze-dried raspberries, crushed with your fingers

Preheat the oven to 100°C/200°F/gas mark low. First make the meringues. Whisk the egg whites until stiff. Gradually whisk in the caster sugar, then add the icing sugar and whisk until combined. Spoon into a piping bag fitted with a 1cm nozzle and pipe six large domes on a baking tray lined with baking parchment. Sprinkle with the freeze-dried raspberries. Place in the oven and dry out for 1 hour, until the outer shell is firm. Remove from the oven. While the meringues are still warm, scoop out all of the soft inside (discard this) so you are left with a shell. Leave to cool.

For the raspberry sauce, put a quarter of the raspberries in a blender and blend to a purée, then pass through a fine sieve (or use frozen raspberries for the sauce, if you prefer).

Lightly whip the cream in a bowl. Break the remaining raspberries in half, then gently fold into the cream together with the raspberry jam and liqueur, if using. Use to fill the meringue shells and serve each on a pool of raspberry sauce.

· YELLOWMAN TOFFEE · CHEESECAKE

Yellowman toffee is an Irish sweet similar to honeycomb. Made by caramelizing sugar and then adding bicarbonate of soda to 'puff' the caramel up, it is quite fun to make. This cheesecake is simple but tastes delicious. We use honey that is gathered from hives on the roofs of high-rise buildings in London.

Serves 8

Yellowman toffee
3 tbsp honey
150g caster or granulated sugar
1 tbsp golden syrup
2 tsp bicarbonate of soda

Cheesecake base
200g digestive biscuits, bashed to crumbs
100g unsalted butter, melted
pinch of salt

Cheesecake filling
500g cream cheese
300ml double cream
4 tbsp runny honey

To make the toffee, put the honey, sugar and golden syrup into a saucepan and heat gently until the sugar has dissolved. Increase the heat and boil rapidly for 3 minutes. Remove from the heat, stir in the bicarbonate of soda and quickly pour on to a greased baking tray. When cool and set, chop into a coarse crumb.

For the cheesecake base, mix the biscuit crumbs and melted butter together with the salt. Press evenly over the bottom of a greased 20cm springform tin. Place in the fridge to firm up.

For the cheesecake filling, put the cream cheese into a mixing bowl. Using an electric mixer, beat at a low speed until smooth. Add half of the cream with the honey and whisk until smooth. Add the remaining cream and whisk until soft peaks form. Add the crushed toffee and whisk until stiff.

Spoon the filling on top of the biscuit base and smooth level with a hot spoon. Place in the fridge and leave to set for at least 2 hours before serving.

· LORD MAYOR'S TRIFLE ·

One of the most popular British puddings, trifle traditionally consists of sponge, fruit, custard and cream. We keep it on the menu all year round, changing the fruit in line with the seasons. The trifle here is flavoured with cherry and coconut. Rhubarb and ginger is another great combination in early spring, when Yorkshire forced rhubarb appears.

Makes 6 individual trifles

Coconut sponge
3 free-range eggs
100g caster sugar
30g cornflour
20g plain flour
50g desiccated coconut, toasted

Begin with the coconut sponge. Preheat the oven to 180°C/350°F/gas mark 4. Butter or spray a 24cm square cake tin and line it with baking parchment. Using an electric mixer, beat the eggs until thick and creamy, then add the sugar and beat until smooth and shiny. Fold in the cornflour, flour and coconut. Pour into the tin. Bake for about 25 minutes, until a skewer inserted into the centre of the sponge comes out clean. Allow to cool on a wire rack, then cut into dice.

Cherries

400g fresh cherries, halved and stoned
25ml cherry juice
25ml Cherry Heering liqueur or kirsch

Cherry jelly

3½ leaves gelatine
400ml cherry juice
50ml Cherry Heering liqueur or kirsch
caster sugar, if needed

Vanilla custard

1 leaf gelatine
100ml milk
100ml double cream
seeds from ½ vanilla pod
40g (about 2) free-range egg yolks
35g caster sugar

Cream

100ml double cream
80ml crème fraîche
25ml Cherry Heering liqueur or kirsch
toasted coconut, to garnish

Mix the cherries with the cherry juice and liqueur.
Set aside to macerate.

For the jelly, soak the gelatine in cold water to soften.
Meanwhile, bring the cherry juice just to the boil and stir in
the liqueur with a little sugar if the juice doesn't taste sweet
enough. Squeeze excess moisture from the gelatine, then add
to the hot juice and stir until melted. Pour the cherry jelly
through a fine sieve into a plastic container (about 24cm
square) and place in the fridge to set. When firm, cut the jelly
into 1cm cubes; keep in the fridge until needed.

To make the custard, soak the gelatine in cold water to soften.
Meanwhile, bring the milk, double cream and vanilla to the
boil in a heavy-based saucepan, then reduce the heat to low.
Whisk the egg yolks and sugar together in a bowl. Pour the
hot cream on to the yolks, mixing well. Pour back into the
pan and cook gently, stirring constantly with a wooden
spoon, until the custard is thick enough to coat the back of
the spoon. Squeeze excess moisture from the gelatine, then
add to the custard and stir until melted. Pour through a fine
sieve into a bowl. Cover and place in the fridge. When the
custard is softly set, beat until smooth, then spoon into a
piping bag fitted with a small plain nozzle. Keep in the fridge.

For the cream, put the double cream, crème fraîche and
liqueur in a bowl and whip until stiff. Place in a piping bag
fitted with a small plain nozzle.

To assemble, mix together the sponge, jelly and cherries with
their liquid, then place in six serving glasses. Pipe the custard
on top and finish with the cream and toasted coconut.

· FLAPJACK ICE CREAM ·

I love flapjacks and I love ice cream, so this is a great
combination for me. I recommend that you make a double
batch of flapjacks so you can cut a few nice bars from it to enjoy
with a cup of tea, and then use the rest for the ice cream!

Serves 6–8

Flapjack
100g unsalted butter
2 tbsp golden syrup
90g light muscovado sugar
150g rolled oats
*50g shelled unsalted peanuts,
roughly chopped*

Ice cream base
300ml whole milk
1 tsp ground cinnamon
4 free-range eggs, separated
150g caster sugar
400ml whipping cream

Preheat the oven to 165°C/325°F/gas mark 3. To make the
flapjack, melt the butter with the syrup and sugar. Add the
oats and peanuts and mix well. Press into a greased and lined
24cm square tin and bake for 20–25 minutes, until golden.
Allow to cool, then chop finely.

For the ice cream base, bring the milk and cinnamon just
to the boil in a heavy-based saucepan; remove from the heat.
Whisk the egg yolks with 50g of the sugar, then whisk in
a little of the hot milk. Add the mix to the hot milk in the
saucepan and cook over a low heat, stirring constantly with
a wooden spoon, until the custard is thick enough to coat
the back of the spoon. Add 100ml of the cream, then pour
through a fine sieve into a shallow container. Cover the
surface of the custard with clingfilm to prevent a skin from
forming and place in the fridge to chill.

Whip the remaining 300ml cream to soft peaks and set aside.
Whisk the egg whites until stiff peaks will form, then add
the remaining 100g sugar and whisk until smooth and glossy.

Fold the custard and whipped cream together, then mix in
the flapjack. Fold in a quarter of the whisked egg whites,
then add the remaining whites and mix gently. Transfer the
mixture to a suitable container for your freezer and cover
with a lid. Freeze for 2–4 hours, until the ice cream is firm
enough to scoop or slice.

· WARM CHOCOLATE IN A POT ·
WITH CHOCOLATE CORNFLAKES

This is a modern version of a traditional English pudding.
The warm, gooey chocolate base is perfectly matched with
its topping of crunchy cornflakes and tangy crème fraîche.
Be sure to use a good-quality dark chocolate.

Makes 6 pots

Chocolate pots mix
*350g dark chocolate (minimum 66% cocoa
solids), roughly chopped*
200ml milk
300ml whipping cream
30g caster sugar
110g (about 6) free-range egg yolks

Chocolate cornflakes
50g milk chocolate, roughly chopped
25g cocoa butter, roughly chopped
100g cornflakes

crème fraîche, to serve

For the chocolate pots mix, put the chopped chocolate into a large bowl and set a clean, dry sieve over it. Combine the milk and cream in a saucepan and bring to the boil, then turn down the heat to low. Whisk together the sugar and egg yolks in a bowl, then add about a quarter of the hot milk mixture, stirring well. Pour this into the remaining milk mixture in the saucepan and cook, stirring constantly with a wooden spoon, until the custard is thick enough to coat the back of the spoon. Pour the mix through the sieve on to the chocolate and leave to melt for a few minutes.

Once the chocolate has melted, blend with a stick blender until the mix is shiny and smooth. Divide among six shallow ramekins that are about 8cm in diameter. Set aside on a baking tray (or keep in the fridge if you are making ahead).

For the cornflakes, melt the chocolate and cocoa butter together in a heatproof bowl set over a pan of gently simmering water. Remove from the heat and fold in the cornflakes. Spread on a tray covered with baking parchment. Place in the fridge to set.

Preheat the oven to 180°C/350°F/gas mark 4. Place the tray of pots in the oven to cook for 3 minutes, then remove and leave to rest in a warm place for 10 minutes. Cover the top of each chocolate pot with chocolate cornflakes and add a dollop of crème fraîche.

· APPLE AMBER ·

Adapted from Mrs Beeton's *Book of Household Management*, this can be made as a large tart or small individual tarts. Apple was the original filling; however, we change this according to what is best in season – fig, pear and apricot all work wonderfully well. In the restaurant, this is served warm with a large dollop of clotted cream.

Makes 1 large or 6 small tarts

Sweet pastry
85g soft unsalted butter
115g caster sugar
225g strong flour
7g baking powder
3g salt
100ml double cream

Apples
6 Granny Smith apples, peeled, cored and cut into eighths
300ml apple juice

Meringue
80g (about 3) fresh free-range egg whites
160g caster sugar

For the sweet pastry, mix the soft butter and sugar together with an electric mixer on slow speed, or in a food processor, until just combined. Sift the flour, baking powder and salt together. Add half to the butter and mix to form a smooth paste, then add the remaining flour and mix just until fine crumbs are formed. Slowly add the cream, mixing just to bind to a dough. Gather into a ball, wrap in clingfilm and place in the fridge to rest for 1 hour.

Roll out the pastry dough between two sheets of baking parchment until 5mm thick. Allow to rest in the fridge again for 20 minutes, then cut into a round to fit in the bottom of your tin or tins. For a large tart, use a 26cm tart tin that is 1.5cm deep; for individual tarts you need six 8cm tart tins that are 1.5cm deep. Line the bottom of the tin (just the bottom, not the sides) with the pastry, then set on a baking tray lined with baking parchment. Place in the fridge to chill while you cook the apples.

Put the apples and apple juice in a large saucepan, set over a moderate heat and cook until just tender. Remove from the heat and cool. Drain the apples in a sieve set over a clean pan; set the apples aside. Boil the apple juice until it has reduced to a thick glaze. Set aside.

Preheat your oven to 180°C/350°F/gas mark 4. Place the tray with the tart tin in the oven and bake for 12 minutes, until the pastry base is set and golden brown. Remove from the oven and reduce the temperature to 165°C/325°F/gas mark 3. Mix the cooked apples with the apple glaze (try not to break down the apples too much so they retain some texture), then pack on top of the pastry in the tin. Bake for 20 minutes, until most of the liquid from the apples has evaporated.

Cover the tart with baking parchment, then set another baking tray on top, weighed down with something heavy, and allow to cool. Once cold, remove the tart from the tin and transfer it to a baking tray.

For the meringue, whisk the egg whites until stiff peaks will form. Gradually add the sugar, whisking, and continue to whisk until very stiff. Place the meringue in a piping bag fitted with a 1.5cm plain nozzle and pipe small 'tufts' on top of the apple. Bake for 6 minutes, until the meringue is crisp on the surface. Serve immediately, or wait until later in the day when the tart will need 5 minutes reheating prior to serving.

·CARAMELIZED BANANA BREAD AND BUTTER PUDDING·

This is a pudding that always gets rave reviews in the restaurant, because it combines three irresistible components: brioche, bananas and custard. When using bananas for baking, they need to be as ripe as possible – the blacker the skins, the more intense the flavour and sweetness of the flesh.

Serves 6

100g golden syrup, plus extra for drizzling
50ml brandy
2 very ripe bananas
soft unsalted butter, for greasing
1 x 400g brioche loaf (or plain white bread
if you prefer), cut into 1cm slices
clotted or pouring cream, to serve
a little melted dark chocolate (optional)

Custard
3 free-range eggs
100ml double cream
300ml milk
50ml brandy

Make the custard first. Beat the eggs well, then add the cream, milk and brandy. Pass through a fine sieve into a jug to remove any lumps of egg. Set aside.

Heat the golden syrup in a pan until it boils and the bubbles get denser. Add the brandy and mix together. Slice the bananas lengthways, then place in the hot caramel. When golden on one side, turn over and caramelize the other side. Remove the pan from the heat.

Preheat the oven to 150°C/300°F/gas mark 2. Line a standard 900g loaf tin with baking parchment and butter well. Make a layer of brioche on the bottom, then pour over enough custard so it is about 1cm above the brioche. Press down on the brioche to help it absorb the custard (the more it soaks up, the moister the pudding will be). When fully soaked in, arrange a layer of sliced bananas on top with the caramel. Repeat the layering until the ingredients are used, finishing with brioche moistened with the last of the custard, allowing it all to soak in. Bake for 30 minutes, until the custard is just set. Allow to cool completely.

When ready to serve, preheat the oven to 200°C/400°F/gas mark 6. Cut the loaf into six slices and lay them out on a well-greased baking tray. Drizzle over a little golden syrup, then bake for 7 minutes. Serve hot, with clotted or pouring cream. (If you like, serve on plates that have been 'painted' with melted chocolate, using a pastry brush.)

· CHOCOLATE RICE KRISPIE ·
SUNDAE

This is a great pudding for both adults and children alike.
The Rice Krispies, coated in chocolate, add a great crunch to
the layers of ice cream and salted caramel sauce. Always use
a good-quality chocolate to ensure the best flavour and texture.

Serves 4

8 scoops good-quality vanilla ice cream

Chocolate Rice Krispie cake
3 tbsp golden syrup
60g unsalted butter
100g milk chocolate, chopped up
90g Rice Krispies
25g toasted coconut

Salted caramel sauce
100g caster sugar
100ml whipping cream
25g unsalted butter
¼ tsp salt

For the chocolate Rice Krispie cake, warm the syrup in a pan, then add the butter and whisk together. Pour this mix over the chocolate and leave to sit for a few minutes, then stir to combine. Fold in the Rice Krispies and coconut. Transfer to a greased standard 900g loaf tin and spread evenly. Place in the fridge to set. When the cake is firm, turn out and chop into rough crumbs for the sundaes.

For the caramel sauce, put the sugar in a pan with enough water to saturate the sugar. Set on a high heat and bring to the boil. Boil until the sugar begins to caramelize. When it is a dark golden colour, carefully add the cream (the mix will spit) and reduce the heat to low. Allow the cream to fully combine with the caramel, stirring, then remove from the heat and whisk in the butter and salt. Pour into a jug and cool, then cover with clingfilm and set aside.

Chill four sundae glasses in the freezer. To assemble the sundaes, layer the ice cream, Rice Krispie crumbs and caramel sauce in the chilled glasses and serve immediately.

· SPOTTED DICK ·

Spotted Dick was created sometime in the mid-19th century – the 'spots' refer to the dried fruit in the pudding. We have slightly adapted the traditional recipe, making it a little more robust in flavour by steeping the fruit in fragrant Earl Grey tea.

Serves 6

250g self-raising flour
pinch of salt
125g shredded suet
100ml milk
custard and ice cream, to serve

Fruit mixture
3 Earl Grey tea bags
75g caster sugar
100ml boiling water
100g currants
50g chopped mixed peel
50g golden raisins
grated zest of 1 orange
grated zest of 1 lemon
1 tsp ground cinnamon
½ tsp ground ginger
1 tbsp freshly grated nutmeg

Put the tea bags in a bowl with the sugar and pour over the boiling water. Allow to steep for 15 minutes, then remove the tea bags. Add the remaining ingredients for the fruit mixture and stir together well. Cover the bowl and leave to macerate overnight.

Drain off any remaining liquid from the fruit. Put the flour, salt and suet in a mixing bowl. Add the milk and macerated fruit and mix to a firm dough.

Turn on to a floured surface and form into a large sausage shape about 18cm long. Wrap very loosely in baking parchment, loosely tying the ends with string. Set a large steamer over a pan of boiling water. Place the pudding in the steamer, cover and steam for 1½ hours, topping up the water when necessary. Allow to cool for 10 minutes, then unwrap and slice to serve with custard and ice cream.

The earliest known mention of a Liverpool Tart was in 1897, when it was hand-written into a family cookery book. It is an interesting recipe – the lemon is boiled until soft, then mixed with butter and sugar and baked in a pastry case.

· LIVERPOOL TART ·

Makes 1 tart

Filling
4 unwaxed lemons
150g unsalted butter
250g caster sugar
2 free-range eggs

Pastry
75g soft unsalted butter
40g icing sugar, sifted
1 free-range egg, beaten
150g plain flour
pinch of salt

Put the whole lemons in a pan of water and bring to a gentle boil, then simmer for 1–2 hours, until soft; drain. Place in a blender or food processor with the butter, sugar and eggs and blend together. Set aside.

For the pastry, cream the butter with the icing sugar in a food processor or with an electric mixer until pale and fluffy. Add the egg, then fold in the flour and salt. Roll out to a round 3mm thick to fit a 26cm tart tin that is 2.5cm deep. Transfer the pastry to a tray and place in the fridge to rest for 20 minutes.

Line the tart tin with the pastry, taking care not to stretch it; reserve the pastry trimmings. Put the tart case in the fridge to rest for 20 minutes.

Preheat the oven to 180°C/350°F/gas mark 4. Line the tart case with baking parchment and fill with baking beans, then bake blind for 25 minutes. Remove the beans and paper. Patch up any holes with the pastry trimmings. Bake for a further 10 minutes.

Reduce the oven temperature to 165°C/325°F/gas mark 3. Fill the tart case with the lemon mixture. Bake for 20–25 minutes, until lightly golden; there should still be a slight wobble in the centre of the filling. Leave to cool before serving.

·KENDAL MINT CAKE·
CHOC ICE

Long used by mountaineers for instant energy, Kendal Mint Cake was carried by Sir Edmund Hillary and his team on their first successful ascent of Mount Everest in 1953. We use it at the restaurant in our popular choc ice (an ice cream bar covered in chocolate), where it gives a minty crunch.

Makes 6

20g Kendal Mint Cake, finely chopped, plus more to garnish if wanted
100g dark chocolate (minimum 70% cocoa solids), broken up

Ice cream base
300ml milk
300ml double cream
25g honey
½ x 400g tin condensed milk
leaves from 25g bunch of mint

Make up the ice cream base by mixing all of the ingredients together in a bowl and blending with a stick blender. Pass through a fine sieve, then churn in your ice cream machine according to the manufacturer's instructions. Scoop into a chilled stainless steel bowl and fold through the mint cake. Place in the freezer to firm up a bit.

Spray six mini loaf tins (3.5 x 9.5 x 6cm) with baking spray, then line the longer sides and the bottom with baking parchment cut exactly to the length of the tin, leaving an overhang that will cover the ice cream. Place the tins in the freezer to chill for 10 minutes.

Stir the ice cream mix again, then spoon into the chilled tins. Using a palette knife, smooth the top, ensuring the mix has gone into all corners and edges. Fold the paper overhang on top of the ice cream. Return to the freezer to freeze solid.

Cut six parchment paper rectangles 9cm wide and 18cm long. Melt the chocolate in a heatproof bowl set over a saucepan of simmering water. Using a palette knife, spread a thin layer of chocolate over each paper rectangle.

One by one, turn the frozen ice cream bars out of the tins and peel off the parchment. Starting 3cm in from the edge of a chocolate rectangle, place the side of the ice cream bar on the chocolate, then roll the ice cream over to wrap up in the chocolate-lined paper. Return to the freezer. When set, carefully peel off the paper and trim the ends using a hot, sharp knife. Garnish the ice cream at the open ends with some microplaned Kendal Mint Cake if you wish.

APRICOT AND ALMOND · CRUMBLE

A crumble is one of the best comfort foods, all year round. The versatile crumble topping here can be used with any fruit in season, as long as it is ripe. And definitely serve with both custard and ice cream!

Serves 4

125g caster sugar
50ml crème d'abricot (apricot liqueur)
or peach schnapps
200ml apricot juice or nectar
1kg fresh apricots, stoned and chopped
custard and ice cream or clotted
cream, to serve

Crumble topping
100g unsalted butter
100g demerara sugar
100g plain flour
100g ground almonds
50g toasted flaked almonds,
finely chopped

For the apricots, put the sugar, liqueur and juice into a saucepan and bring to the boil. Turn down the heat, then add the chopped apricots. Cover and simmer for 5 minutes. Remove from the heat and set aside, covered, for 20 minutes.

For the crumble, cream the butter with the sugar, then mix in the other ingredients to make a crumbly texture.

Preheat the oven to 180°C/350°F/gas mark 4. Place the apricot mix in a baking dish and cover with the crumble topping. Bake for 20–30 minutes, until the crumble is golden and the fruit bubbling. Serve with custard and ice cream or clotted cream.

·CAMBRIDGE BURNT CREAM·

Some say that this dish originated at Trinity College, Cambridge in 1879, with the college arms 'impressed on top of the cream with a branding iron'. However, the French are insistent that their version, crème brûlée, is the original. Either way, it's a wonderful pudding.

Makes 6

250ml milk
250ml double cream
110g (about 6) free-range egg yolks
40g dark muscovado sugar
40g caster sugar
6 tsp demerara sugar

Preheat the oven to 120°C/250°F/gas mark ½. Place six ramekins in a deep baking tray.

Put the milk and cream in a heavy-based saucepan and bring to a simmer, then turn the heat down. Whisk the egg yolks with the muscovado and caster sugars, just to mix. Add a little of the hot cream, then pour this into the rest of the hot cream in the pan. Cook, stirring constantly with a wooden spoon, until the custard is thick enough to coat the back of the spoon. Pour the custard through a fine sieve into a jug; skim off any foam.

Pour enough boiling water into the baking tray, around the ramekins, to half fill the tray. Fill the ramekins evenly with the custard. Cover the entire tray with foil and place in the oven to cook for 20 minutes. Remove the foil and check the consistency of the creams: they should be set but with a slight wobble in the centre. Remove from the tray of hot water and cool, then place in the fridge to chill. Remove the creams from the fridge 1 hour before required.

If you aren't going to use a blowtorch, preheat the grill to high. Set the ramekins in the empty baking tray and surround with ice. Sprinkle 1 teaspoon of demerara sugar over the surface of each cream. Melt and caramelize the sugar with a blowtorch or very quickly under the grill. Allow the caramel to cool and set for a few minutes, then serve.

· LEMON CREAM ICE ·
WITH SALTED CARAMEL POPCORN

Our adaptation of a recipe in Mrs Beeton's *Book of Household Management* still calls this a cream ice, although in modern day terms we would describe it as a parfait. It works superbly well with the sweet saltiness of the crunchy popcorn.

Serves 8

Salted caramel popcorn
40g popcorn kernels
vegetable oil, for popping (if needed)
100g caster sugar
50g unsalted butter
¼ tsp salt

Cream ice
grated zest and juice of 1 lemon
150ml double cream, lightly whipped
200g caster or granulated sugar
100ml water
3 free-range eggs, 2 of them separated

good-quality purchased lemon curd,
to serve

Pop the popcorn following the manufacturer's instructions for your popcorn-popper, or pop in a little oil in a covered saucepan. Sort through to remove any unpopped kernels.

Melt the sugar in a medium-sized saucepan over a moderate heat and cook until it begins to caramelize. Swirl the pan to ensure it colours evenly, then whisk in the butter and salt. Add the popcorn and mix well with a spatula to coat evenly. Pour on to a sheet of baking parchment and pull the popcorn apart with two forks as it cools to create individual pieces.

For the cream ice, gently fold the lemon zest and juice into the whipped cream in a large bowl; set aside. Put 100g of the sugar and 50ml of the water in a pan and bring to a rapid boil, then boil for 3 minutes. Meanwhile, slowly whisk the 2 egg whites in a large electric mixer until stiff. Gradually whisk in the hot sugar syrup to create a glossy meringue. Continue whisking until cool, then set aside.

Make another batch of sugar syrup with the remaining sugar and water. Put the whole egg and 2 egg yolks in another bowl and whisk together, then whisk in the hot syrup; continue whisking until cool. Carefully fold the meringue into the whipped cream, then add the yolk mixture. Spoon into a small (450g) loaf tin lined with baking parchment. Place in the freezer to firm up for at least 3 hours, until frozen solid.

To serve, chop the caramel popcorn into a coarse crumb. Remove the cream ice from the loaf tin and peel off the lining paper. Coat the top and bottom of the cream ice evenly with popcorn, then slice. Serve immediately, with a dragged spoonful of lemon curd on the plate next to the cream ice.

·GOOSEBERRY· UPSIDE-DOWN PUDDING

I think gooseberries are one of Britain's finest fruits.
Their tartness works perfectly in this pudding, balancing
the sweet buttery caramel that surrounds them on top of
the golden sponge. Serve hot with pouring cream.

Serves 4

100g soft unsalted butter
100g caster sugar
400g gooseberries (fresh or frozen)
pouring cream, to serve

Pudding mix
100g unsalted butter
100g light muscovado sugar
2 free-range eggs, beaten
200g self-raising flour
½ tsp salt

Preheat the oven to 180°C/350°F/gas mark 4. Using your knuckles, evenly spread the soft butter over the bottom of a 20cm baking dish. Sprinkle the sugar evenly on top, then add the gooseberries.

For the pudding mix, cream the butter with the sugar until light and fluffy. Add the eggs, mixing well, then fold in the flour and salt. Spread over the gooseberries. Bake for 20–25 minutes, until golden and a skewer inserted into the centre comes out clean. Cool for 5 minutes, then turn out on to a serving dish and serve hot.

· BLACKBERRY ·
ETON MESS SUNDAE

This is a take on the classic Eton Mess, turning it into a sundae. It must be made with perfectly ripe fruit to ensure that the meringue, whipped cream, ice cream and fruit all combine to create a perfect pudding.

Serves 4

2 tbsp blackberry jam
50ml crème de mûre (blackberry liqueur)
350g ripe blackberries, halved
150ml whipping or double cream, whipped
8 scoops Cornish vanilla ice cream
4 meringues, crushed
freeze-dried blackberries (optional)

Whisk the jam with the blackberry liqueur in a bowl. Add the blackberries and mix gently, then set aside to macerate for at least 1 hour.

Assemble the sundaes in chilled sundae glasses with layers of blackberries, cream, ice cream and meringue. Decorate with freeze-dried blackberries, if you wish.

· TREACLE TART ·

According to my children, treacle tart is Harry Potter's favourite dessert.
I would agree with him – this sticky sweet tart is a great way to finish off
a meal, or to have with a cup of tea in the afternoon.

Makes 1 tart

Pastry
75g soft unsalted butter
40g icing sugar, sifted
1 free-range egg, beaten
150g plain flour
pinch of salt

Filling
250g golden syrup
90g black treacle
85g fresh white breadcrumbs
60g ground almonds
1 free-range egg
100ml double cream

Begin by making the pastry. Cream the butter with the icing sugar in a food processor or with an electric mixer until pale and fluffy. Mix in the egg, then fold in the flour and salt. Shape into a ball and wrap in clingfilm, then place in the fridge to rest for 25 minutes.

Roll out the pastry 3mm thick to fit a 25cm tart tin that is 4cm deep. Transfer the pastry to a tray and return to the fridge to rest for 20 minutes. Line the tin with the pastry, taking care not to stretch it; reserve the pastry trimmings. Return to the fridge to rest again for 20 minutes.

Preheat the oven to 180°C/350°F/gas mark 4. Line the tart case with baking parchment and fill with baking beans, then bake blind for 30 minutes. Remove the beans and paper, and patch up any holes with the pastry trimmings. Bake for a further 10 minutes. Remove from the oven; leave the oven on.

Heat the syrups, then remove from the heat and add all of the other filling ingredients. Set aside for 10 minutes, then pour into the tart case. Bake for 20–25 minutes, until just set in the centre. Serve warm or cool.

· GINGERBREAD PUDDING ·

A real warming winter pudding, this is very simple to make. The addition of pear ensures it is moist, and stem ginger gives it a little kick.

Serves 6

120g soft unsalted butter
50g caster sugar
100g golden syrup
3 free-range eggs
1 tbsp ground ginger
½ tsp ground cinnamon
50g stem ginger in syrup, finely chopped
1 ripe but firm pear, peeled and grated
50ml milk
½ tsp bicarbonate of soda
100g self-raising flour
clotted cream or ice cream, to serve

Caramel sauce
50g unsalted butter
50g golden syrup
50ml water

Preheat the oven to 165°C/325°F/gas mark 3. Cream the butter with the sugar until light and fluffy. Add the syrup, eggs, ground ginger, cinnamon, chopped ginger and pear and mix well. Heat the milk and stir in the bicarbonate of soda. Add to the ginger mix, then fold in the flour until just combined. Set aside.

For the sauce, melt the butter and syrup together, then add the water and whisk well. Pour into the bottom of a 20cm diameter (or thereabouts) baking dish. Carefully scrape the ginger pudding mix into the dish. Place in the oven and bake for 20–25 minutes, until a skewer inserted into the centre comes out clean. Allow to cool for 10 minutes before serving with clotted cream or ice cream.

· RHUBARB KNICKERBOCKER · GLORY

Super sweet and tender, Yorkshire forced rhubarb is one of Britain's finest products. Only grown in the 'Yorkshire triangle', the rhubarb is in season at the beginning of the year, which is a perfect time to enjoy this great dessert. Use a top-quality ice cream for the best result.

Serves 4

150ml double cream
25ml Amaretto Disaronno (almond liqueur)
12 small scoops good-quality vanilla ice cream

Almond meringue
70g (about 2½) free-range egg whites
100g caster sugar
25g flaked almonds, toasted and finely chopped

Rhubarb
200g caster sugar
250ml water
1 tbsp rose water
1 tsp grenadine
4 sticks rhubarb, cut into 1cm pieces

Begin with the meringue. Preheat the oven to 150°C/300°F/gas mark 2. Whisk the egg whites until stiff, then slowly whisk in the sugar and continue whisking until the sugar has been absorbed (you should feel no grains when you rub a little of the meringue between your fingers) and the meringue is glossy. Fold through the chopped almonds. Dollop in eight mounds on a baking tray lined with baking parchment. Place in the oven and bake for 25 minutes, then turn off the oven and leave the meringues inside to dry for a further hour. Remove and leave to cool.

For the rhubarb, put the sugar, water, rose water and grenadine in a pan and bring to the boil. Reduce the heat to a very gentle simmer, then add the rhubarb. Cover with a lid and poach for 5 minutes, until tender. Lift out the rhubarb with a slotted spoon. Put half of it in a container and the rest into a blender. Add 2 tablespoons of the poaching syrup to the blender and pour the rest over the rhubarb in the container; leave to cool. Purée the rhubarb in the blender to make a rhubarb sauce. Place the poached rhubarb and the sauce in the fridge to chill.

Whip the cream with the Amaretto until soft peaks form.

To assemble, layer the ice cream, poached rhubarb and rhubarb sauce, cream and crushed meringue in four chilled sundae glasses, then serve immediately.

· RASPBERRY ROLY POLY ·

I remember having Roly Poly pudding, with lashings of thick custard, when I was a child at school. I'm still fond of it today, although now prefer a big scoop of clotted cream on the side.

Serves 6

250g self-raising flour
½ tsp salt
50g soft light brown sugar
125g shredded suet
100g raspberry jam
50ml milk
1 tbsp demerara sugar
custard, clotted cream or ice cream,
to serve

Preheat the oven to 130°C/250°F/gas mark ½. Prepare a deep roasting tray with a baking rack that fits inside. Elevate the rack by using foil scrunched into balls, or metal baking rings, to ensure you can put 3cm of water in the bottom of the tray.

Mix together the flour, salt, sugar and suet. Add enough cold water to bind the ingredients to create a stiff, not sticky, dough. Roll out on a floured surface to a rectangle 1cm thick. Spread over the jam, leaving a 2cm border clear at one of the longer edges. Brush the edge without jam with milk. Roll up from the opposite long edge and press the join to seal. Brush the roll with the remaining milk and sprinkle with the demerara sugar.

Cut a good length of baking parchment and make a 2cm fold in the centre. Very loosely roll up the roly poly in the paper and loosely tie the ends with string. Pour boiling water into the roasting tray to a depth of 3cm. Set the wrapped roly poly on the rack. Cover the entire tray with foil. Place in the oven to steam for 3 hours.

Remove the pudding and allow to cool for 10 minutes, then unwrap and serve with your choice of custard, clotted cream and ice cream, or all three!

· SUSSEX POND PUDDING ·

Some say this pudding is so-named because when you break it open, a 'pond' forms around it from the lemon caramel centre.

**Makes 1 large pudding
or 4 small puddings**

Suet pastry
250g self-raising flour
125g shredded suet
pinch of salt
160ml water
milk, for brushing

Filling
250g soft unsalted butter
250g light muscovado sugar
1 unwaxed lemon

For the pastry, mix the flour, suet and salt together, then add the water to bind to a dough. Wrap in clingfilm and allow to rest for 20 minutes.

Meanwhile, cream the butter with the sugar until light and fluffy. Set aside.

Butter or spray the moulds you are using – a 1.1 litre mould for a large pudding or four 275ml moulds for individual puddings – then prepare your steamer.

If making a large pudding, divide the pastry into two unequal portions – one about a quarter of the pastry and the other the remaining three-quarters. Roll out into two rounds, the large one to line the mould and the other for the lid. If you are making four individual puddings, first divide the pastry into four and then each quarter into two unequal portions. Line the mould or moulds, ensuring there are no air bubbles.

For a large pudding, prick the lemon all over; for individual puddings, trim off the ends from the lemon, then cut across into four slices. Half fill the pastry case with the butter mix, then add the lemon. Cover with the remaining butter mix, packing it in well.

Brush the edge of the pastry case with milk, then set the lid on top and seal the edge firmly. Cover with a double layer of greaseproof paper and a single sheet of foil. Tie around the top edge with string, securing tightly. Steam for 3 hours. Allow to cool slightly before turning out to serve.

· JAFFA CAKE PUDDINGS ·

I will share a secret with you: Jaffa Cakes are one of my favourite treats, which is why Chantelle created this dessert. It had to go on the menu from opening day. We serve it with an Earl Grey tea ice cream, so it is like having afternoon tea (tea and cake) for pudding.

Makes 8

Chocolate orange ganache
50g good-quality dark chocolate (orange-flavoured, if available), chopped
50ml whipping cream
splash of Cointreau

Candied orange
1 unwaxed orange, scrubbed
2 tbsp marmalade
1 tbsp water

Cake
100g soft unsalted butter
8g grated orange zest
180g caster sugar
2 free-range eggs
60ml soured cream
90g plain flour
5g baking powder

Begin with the ganache. Put the chopped chocolate in a bowl. Heat the cream with the Cointreau until boiling, then pour over the chocolate. Cover with clingfilm and set aside for 5 minutes, then whisk together. If you want to pipe the ganache, spoon into a piping bag fitted with a small plain nozzle. Or just cover the bowl. Leave at room temperature.

For the candied orange, cut the orange, from top to bottom, into quarters. Cut these across into slices 2mm thick. Put the marmalade and water into a shallow saucepan and bring to a simmer. Add the orange slices, cover with a disc of baking parchment and simmer very gently for 25 minutes. Use a slotted spoon to lift out the orange slices. Carefully strain the liquid and reserve. Line eight greased 8cm half-sphere moulds with the slices – three slices per mould.

Preheat the oven to 160°C/325°F/gas mark 3. For the cake, beat the butter with the orange zest and sugar in an electric mixer until creamy. Lightly beat the eggs and soured cream together, then add to the butter mixture, beating well. Sift the flour with the baking powder, then fold into the egg mixture. Divide among the orange-lined moulds. Bake for 20 minutes, until a skewer inserted into the centre comes out clean. Allow to cool slightly in the moulds.

Turn out the cakes. Spoon the reserved marmalade syrup into the moulds, then replace the cakes. Leave to cool completely; the cakes will absorb the syrup.

Cut out about a 2cm plug from the centre of each cake. Pipe or spoon in the ganache, then replace the plug. Before serving, turn out the cakes on to a baking tray lined with baking parchment and reheat in a 150°C/300°F/gas mark 2 oven for 5 minutes to melt the ganache.

· PEACH MELBA ·

This is a British classic, created in the 1890s at the Savoy Hotel in London to honour the Australian opera singer, Dame Nellie Melba. It is at its best when made in summer as it combines two great summer fruits: peaches and raspberries.

Serves 4

4 scoops good-quality vanilla ice cream

Poached peaches
150g caster sugar
150ml water
2 star anise
50ml crème de pêche (peach liqueur)
or peach schnapps
1 vanilla pod, split lengthways
2 white peaches, halved and stoned

Candied almonds
50g flaked almonds
1 tbsp caster sugar
pinch of salt

Raspberry sauce
175g fresh raspberries (or frozen
if fresh are not available)
icing sugar

For the peaches, put the sugar, water, star anise and liqueur in a saucepan just big enough to fit the four peach halves in one layer. Scrape the seeds from the vanilla pod and add to the pan along with the empty pod. Bring to the boil, then reduce to a gentle simmer and add the peaches (they should be immersed in the syrup). Cover with a lid and gently poach for 15–20 minutes, until the peaches are just tender. Using a slotted spoon, remove the peach halves from the syrup and slip off the skins. Place in a container and cool. Leave the syrup to cool also. When both are cold, pour the syrup over the peaches, then keep in the fridge until needed; drain the peaches before using (you can add soda water to the syrup to make a delicious drink).

Preheat the oven to 180°C/350°F/gas mark 4. To make the candied almonds, moisten the almonds with a splash of water, then add the sugar and salt and toss to coat. Spread out on a baking tray lined with baking parchment and bake for 5–8 minutes, until golden. Allow to cool.

For the raspberry sauce, blend the raspberries to a purée. Pass through a fine sieve into a bowl. Stir in enough icing sugar to make a slightly sweet, but still tart, sauce.

About 10 minutes before you want to serve the dessert, make the scoops of ice cream and return to the freezer on a tray.

Cut a small dip in the curved side of each peach half, so the ice cream can sit on it securely. To assemble the desserts, divide the raspberry sauce among four serving bowls, then place the peach halves, flat side down, on the sauce. Set an ice cream scoop on top of each peach half. Finish by scattering over the almonds.

BRUNCH

When we started serving brunch at The Gilbert Scott we wanted
to devise a menu that had a good balance of robust and light dishes,
both sweet and savoury, which could be enjoyed at any time from an
early breakfast through to lunch. I think we have succeeded.

You can judge for yourself by trying some of our brunch dishes
in this chapter. They range from eggy bread and toasted muesli to
corned beef hash and crab 'Benedict'. And of course I had to include
our version of the Full English Breakfast, with bacon, eggs, sausages,
black pudding, home-made baked beans, bubble and squeak cakes,
and toast on the side – a veritable feast!

· HOME-MADE · TOASTED MUSELI

This is simple to make, and you can add or substitute your favourite dried fruit or nuts. It can be kept for a good few weeks, if you can resist temptation that is!

Makes 12 servings

150g honey
50ml groundnut oil
500g rolled oats
80g wheatgerm
60g desiccated coconut
60g bran flakes
80g sesame seeds
80g pumpkin seeds
80g whole, skin-on almonds, roughly chopped
100g pitted prunes, diced
100g dried apricots, diced

Preheat the oven to 140°C/275°F/gas mark 1. Gently warm the honey and oil in a saucepan. Combine the remaining ingredients, except the fruit, in a large bowl. Pour the honey and oil mix over and stir to coat everything.

Spread out in a large roasting tray and bake for 15 minutes, stirring regularly. Stir in the fruit and cook for a further 10 minutes, until lightly golden. Allow to cool, then keep in an airtight container (for up to 2 weeks).

· BACON FLODDIES ·

Floddies are grated potato, bacon and onion cakes traditional to the Tyneside town of Gateshead, where it is said they were cooked by the canal workers on shovels over a fire. They're delicious with sausages and eggs as a breakfast or supper dish.

Serves 4

225g peeled potatoes (preferably waxy)
2 onions, peeled and finely chopped
or grated
150g rashers smoked streaky bacon,
finely chopped
50g self-raising flour
2 free-range eggs, beaten
4 tbsp vegetable oil, or 40g bacon fat

Grate the potatoes on to a board. Squeeze out excess liquid, then place in a bowl. Add the onions, bacon, flour and seasoning. Mix very well together. Stir in the eggs.

Fry the floddies in batches. Heat the oil or bacon fat in a large frying pan. Put heaped tablespoonfuls of the mixture into the pan, spaced apart, and fry for 5–8 minutes, turning once, until golden brown and cooked through. Drain on kitchen paper and keep hot until all the floddies have been cooked. Serve hot.

· BRUMMIE BACON CAKES ·

This is a recipe from an old Women's Institute cookery book and originated in the city of Birmingham. The scone-like cakes are great for brunch or as a snack with a good cup of English tea.

Serves 4

50g rashers streaky bacon
225g self-raising flour
¼ tsp salt
25g cold butter
75g Cheddar cheese, grated
150ml milk, plus extra for glazing
1 tbsp tomato ketchup
dash of Worcestershire sauce

Preheat the oven to 200°C/400°F/gas mark 6. Grill or fry the bacon until crisp, then cut into small pieces. Sift the flour and salt into a bowl and rub in the butter to make a fine crumb texture. Add the bacon and a third of the cheese.

Mix together the milk, ketchup and Worcestershire sauce in a separate bowl. Add to the bacon mixture and briefly mix to make a soft dough. Roll out on a floured board to an 18cm round. Brush with milk, then cut into eight wedges.

Arrange the wedges on a greased baking sheet and sprinkle with the remaining cheese. Bake for 30 minutes, until risen and golden brown. Serve hot, or cool on a wire rack and keep in an airtight container.

·OATMEAL FRITTERS·

These are dense and slightly nutty-tasting griddle cakes, great for using up any leftover porridge. I like them with lashings of maple syrup, plus some Devonshire clotted cream for the ultimate treat.

Serves 4

250ml milk
100g rolled oats
½ tsp salt
3 free-range eggs, beaten
50g butter

Bring the milk to a simmer, then add the oats and cook gently, stirring occasionally, for 5–6 minutes. Transfer to a mixing bowl, cover and allow to cool for 20 minutes. Then beat in the salt and eggs.

Cook the fritters in batches. Melt some of the butter in a frying pan. When hot and foaming, add spoonfuls of the oats mix and cook for about 4 minutes on each side, until golden brown. Remove from the pan and keep hot. Continue frying the fritters, adding more butter as needed. Serve with maple syrup or honey, fruit and icing sugar, or bacon and eggs.

Oatmeal Fritters are pictured with the Full English Breakfast on page 208.

· CORNED BEEF HASH ·
WITH FRIED DUCK EGG

This is a great weekend breakfast or lunch dish. Duck eggs
are slightly larger than hen's eggs so you get more of the
yolk to intensify the flavour and colour of the dish.

Serves 4

2 medium waxy potatoes, peeled and chopped
25g unsalted butter
1 onion, peeled and finely sliced
1 free-range egg, beaten
leaves from ¼ bunch of flat-leaf
parsley, chopped
2 tbsp Worcestershire sauce
dash of Tabasco sauce
½ tsp salt
freshly ground black pepper to taste
300g good-quality corned beef, at
room temperature, broken up
into chunks
plain flour, for dusting
2 tbsp vegetable oil
10g unsalted butter

Duck eggs
1 tbsp vegetable oil
4 duck eggs
Maldon sea salt

Put the potatoes into a pan of salted water and bring to
the boil. Cook until tender, then drain and leave to cool to
room temperature. Meanwhile, heat the butter in a frying
pan and add the onion. Season and fry until golden. Remove
from the heat.

Divide the potatoes in half, mashing one half and lightly
crushing the other. Add the egg to the mashed potato along
with the onion, parsley, Worcestershire and Tabasco sauces,
salt and some pepper.

Fold the corned beef and crushed potato into the mashed
potato mix. Shape into four patties and dust with flour.
Heat the vegetable oil in a frying pan and brown the patties
on both sides. Add the butter and continue cooking for
about 5 minutes, until heated through. Keep warm while
you cook the duck eggs.

Heat the oil in a frying pan over a moderately high heat.
Break in the eggs and gently fry until they are cooked to
your liking. Season with sea salt and serve with the patties.

· BANANA EGGY BREAD ·
WITH BACON

The English version of French Toast, eggy bread is one of those dishes that conjures up happy childhood memories. If you've not tried the sweet and salty combination of banana, bacon and maple syrup before then I do hope you enjoy it as much as our customers do.

Serves 4

3 free-range eggs
250ml milk
1 unsliced loaf of your favourite bread
2 ripe bananas, mashed together
2 tbsp vegetable oil
50g unsalted butter
1 banana, sliced
100ml maple syrup
8 rashers streaky bacon, grilled
until crisp, to serve

Beat the eggs with the milk in a shallow, wide dish. Cut eight 2cm-thick slices from the loaf. Lay four slices of bread on the work surface. Divide the mashed banana among the slices and spread evenly, leaving a 1cm edge uncovered on all sides. Brush the edge with a little of the egg mix, then place the other slices of bread on top and press down to seal. Place the 'sandwiches' into the egg mix and allow to soak well on both sides until all the egg mix has been absorbed.

Heat a large frying pan with 1 tablespoon of the vegetable oil over a moderate heat. Place two of the sandwiches in the pan and brown on both sides, then add 15g of the butter and brown further. Remove and keep hot. Clean the pan, then repeat the process with the remaining two sandwiches, the rest of the oil and another 15g butter.

Clean the pan, then melt the remaining butter in it. Add the sliced banana and brown well. Add the maple syrup and swirl to mix. Top the eggy bread with the bananas in syrup and hot bacon and serve immediately.

· FULL ENGLISH BREAKFAST ·

W. Somerset Maugham, a great British playwright and novelist, said,
'To eat well in England you should have breakfast three times a day.'
The 'Full English' has many variations. This is our version.

Serves 4

Spice mix for black pudding

1 star anise
5g whole allspice
1 tsp ground ginger
½ tsp freshly grated nutmeg
3g coriander seeds
5g white peppercorns
2 cloves

Black pudding

50g porridge oats
300ml fresh pig's blood
200g lardo, finely diced
60g butter
1 onion, peeled and finely diced
*1 Granny Smith apple, peeled, cored
and cut into 1cm dice*
50ml Calvados
½ bunch of chives, chopped
1 free-range egg, lightly beaten
a little vegetable oil, for frying

Start with the black pudding. Preheat the oven to 130°C/250°F/gas mark ½. For the spice mix, place all the spices in a spice mill or clean coffee grinder and grind to a fine powder. Set aside.

Mix the oats into the pig's blood in a bowl and leave to soak while you get the rest of the ingredients ready. Put the lardo in a pan of cold water, bring to a gentle simmer and blanch for 20 minutes; drain and leave to cool to room temperature. Heat 15g of the butter in a pan and cook the onion until soft, without browning. In another pan, melt 15g butter and, when foaming, add the apple and cook for a few minutes. Stir in the Calvados and cook for a further 2 minutes. Remove the onion and apple from the heat and allow to cool.

Add the lardo, onion, apple mix and chives to the oats. Mix in the egg. Season with the spice mix, some salt and lots of pepper. Cook a small amount of the mix in hot oil in a frying pan to check the seasoning; adjust if necessary. Line a 22 x 10cm loaf tin with two layers of foil, then spoon in the black pudding mix. Smooth the top, then cover the tin with foil and set in a baking dish. Pour warm water into the dish to fill it by a quarter. Place in the oven and bake for about 30 minutes. To test if the pudding is cooked, insert a probe instant-read thermometer into the centre: it should register 74°C.

Remove the tin from the bain marie. Set something heavy on top of the pudding to press it down evenly and allow to cool, then chill for at least 4 hours before slicing to serve.

Smoky baked beans

100g dried white beans, soaked
overnight and drained
2 tbsp pomace oil
¼ onion, peeled and finely diced
1 clove garlic, peeled and crushed
1 chilli, finely chopped
25ml white wine vinegar
1 tbsp black treacle
1 tsp tomato purée
150g tinned chopped tomatoes
200ml tomato juice
100g smoked bacon lardons

Bubble and squeak cakes

25g butter
¼ onion, peeled and finely sliced
1 tbsp extra virgin olive oil
200g leftover cooked vegetables, chopped (or
50g each mashed potato; finely sliced
cabbage, cooked in butter;
chopped roasted carrots; and
chopped roasted swede)
1 tbsp chopped flat-leaf parsley
plain flour, for coating
vegetable oil, for frying

To serve

8–12 rashers smoked streaky bacon
4 good-quality pork sausages
4–8 free-range eggs
butter, for frying
slices of your favourite bread,
toasted and hot

Next make the baked beans. Put the soaked beans in a pan, cover with water and bring to the boil. Cook for about 25 minutes, then drain. Preheat the oven to 150°C/300°F/ gas mark 2. Heat the oil in a pan, add the onion, garlic and chilli and cook until soft. Add the vinegar, treacle, tomato purée and tinned tomatoes and bring to the boil. Add the beans, tomato juice, bacon and some seasoning, stirring well to mix. Pour into a baking dish, cover with foil and place in the oven. Bake for 25–35 minutes, until the beans are tender. Set aside in a pan, ready to reheat for serving.

For the bubble and squeak cakes, heat a frying pan and add the butter. When foaming, add the onion with a pinch of salt and cook until golden. Add the oil, then transfer to a mixing bowl and add the cooked vegetables. Season well and add the chopped parsley. Mix together. Shape into four small patties. Set aside in a cool place.

The key to a great breakfast is to ensure everything is hot and ready to go at the same time. When ready to serve put the pan of baked beans over a low heat and leave to warm through. Meanwhile, fry or grill the bacon and sausages; keep hot in a warm oven. Coat the bubble and squeak cakes with flour, then fry in a little vegetable oil until golden brown on both sides and heated through; keep hot in the oven. Fry the black pudding slices in the remaining 30g butter until hot, turning once. Finally, fry the eggs in butter until cooked to your liking. Assemble everything on hot plates and serve with toast.

· DORSET CRAB 'BENEDICT' ·

This has been the most popular dish on our brunch menu since introduced in 2012. The saltiness of the crab is the perfect foil to the rich, unctous hollandaise. A great dish to have with a glass of English sparkling wine for a decadent start to your day.

Serves 2

Hollandaise
1 small shallot, peeled and sliced
1 clove garlic, peeled and sliced
1 bay leaf
3 coriander seeds
2 white peppercorns
1 sprig tarragon
100ml white wine vinegar
3 free-range egg yolks
125g unsalted butter, melted

Crab mix
25g brown crab meat
1 tbsp good-quality purchased mayonnaise
100g picked white crab meat
1 tsp lemon juice

dash of white wine vinegar
2 free-range eggs, for poaching
2 English muffins, toasted

Start by making the reduction for the hollandaise. Place all of the ingredients, except the yolks and butter, in a small pan and bring to the boil. Simmer rapidly until the liquid has reduced by just over half. Strain through a fine sieve and set the liquid aside; discard the ingredients in the sieve.

Whisk the brown crab meat into the mayonnaise until smooth, then add the white crab meat, a touch of lemon juice, and seasoning to taste, mixing well. Taste to ensure the seasoning is correct. Set aside.

Put the egg yolks for the hollandaise in a heatproof bowl and set over a pan of gently simmering water. Whisk the yolks until soft and fluffy. Slowly drizzle the melted butter into the yolks, whisking well. When the mix has thickened, add a little of the reduction to taste. Season. Remove the bowl from the pan of water, cover with clingfilm and set aside in a warm place.

Bring a medium saucepan of water to the boil. Add a pinch of salt and a dash of white wine vinegar. Crack each egg into a teacup. Whisk the water, to get it moving in the pan, then gently pour in the eggs, one by one. Poach until cooked to your taste, then remove with a slotted spoon and drain briefly on kitchen paper.

Place the toasted muffins on plates and divide the crab mix between them. Top with the poached eggs, then spoon on the hollandaise. Serve immediately.

·RICOTTA GRIDDLE CAKES·
WITH BLACKCURRANTS

These have a fantastic creamy texture. You can replace the blackcurrants
with any seasonal fruit – poached rhubarb is especially good.

Serves 4

2 tbsp blackcurrant jam
200g blackcurrants (fresh or thawed frozen)
icing sugar, for dusting

Griddle cakes
250g ricotta
3 free-range eggs, separated
80g self-raising flour
pinch of salt
50g unsalted butter

Warm the jam in a saucepan, then add the blackcurrants and
stir in gently. Remove from the heat, cover and keep warm.

Mix together the ricotta, egg yolks, flour and salt in a bowl.
Whisk the egg whites in another bowl until stiff, then gently
fold into the ricotta mix.

You will probably have to cook the griddle cakes in batches.
Heat some of the butter in a griddle or frying pan. Add
spoonfuls of the batter, leaving space around them, and fry
for 3–4 minutes on each side, until lightly golden and cooked
through. Remove from the pan and keep warm. Fry the
remaining griddle cakes, adding more butter as needed.

Dust the cakes with icing sugar and serve with the warm
blackcurrant sauce.

· SAVOURY BAKED EGGS ·

Always try to use free-range eggs when eggs are the
main part of a dish. The yolks will be a beautiful orange
colour and packed with creamy flavour too.

Serves 2

2 tbsp extra virgin olive oil
4 large free-range eggs
½ tsp Maldon sea salt
½ tsp coarsely ground black pepper
1 tbsp chopped tarragon
20g Gruyère cheese, grated
4 tbsp double cream

Preheat the oven to 165°C/325°F/gas mark 3. Divide the
olive oil between two shallow ramekins and crack two eggs
into each one. Season the eggs, then sprinkle with the
tarragon and cheese. Spoon the cream on top.

Set the ramekins in a roasting tray a quarter filled with hot
water. Carefully place in the oven and bake for 6–8 minutes,
until the eggs are still a bit wobbly, or cooked to your taste.
Serve immediately.

OMELETTE ARNOLD BENNETT·

I began my cookery career at The Savoy so this recipe has quite a lot of significance for me. The English writer Arnold Bennett (born in 1867) stayed at The Savoy while writing one of his novels, and he requested this dish be made for him. Since then it has become a staple on the menu there, appropriately named. It is a decadent dish but very, very tasty.

Serves 4

6 free-range eggs
1 tbsp vegetable oil
75g Gruyère cheese, grated

Haddock
200ml milk
2 bay leaves
3 sprigs thyme
160g undyed smoked haddock fillet

Sauce
½ onion, peeled and sliced
2 cloves garlic, peeled and chopped
3 sprigs thyme
1 bay leaf
4 white peppercorns
100ml Noilly Prat vermouth
50ml double cream
2 free-range egg yolks
150g butter, melted
50ml double cream, whipped

Begin by cooking the haddock. Heat the milk with the herbs in a wide pan to a gentle simmer. Add the haddock and poach for 5–8 minutes, until cooked through. Lift out of the milk (discard this). Remove the skin and flake the fish, keeping it in large chunks. Set aside.

To make the sauce, put the onion, garlic, thyme, bay leaf and peppercorns into a pan with the Noilly Prat. Bring to the boil, then reduce the vermouth to a syrup. Add the cream and bring back to a simmer, then remove from the heat, cover and leave for 20 minutes. Pass through a fine sieve into a bowl or jug and set aside.

Place the egg yolks in a heatproof mixing bowl and set over a large saucepan of gently simmering water. Whisk the yolks until light and fluffy. Slowly add the melted butter, whisking constantly. When all the butter has been incorporated and the mixture is thick, add the vermouth reduction and season to taste. Remove from the pan of hot water and finish by folding in the whipped cream. Set aside somewhere warm.

Preheat your grill to as hot as possible. Lightly beat the eggs, seasoning them well. Heat an ovenproof frying pan, about 25cm in diameter, with the oil, then pour in the egg mix and cook, stirring slowly, until the eggs are just beginning to set. Add the haddock and stir through, followed by the cheese. Spread out the egg mix again, then gently cover with the sauce, smoothing it over. Place the pan under the grill and cook until the top of the omelette is a deep golden colour. Serve immediately.

· DYETT BREAD ·

Based on a traditional Tudor recipe, this bread contains an unusual flavouring of fennel and sage. At the restaurant we serve it with another Tudor-inspired bread called Maslin. Dyett bread was eaten by the wealthy – it is made mainly with white flour, which was more expensive than less refined flours in Tudor times. It smells wonderful while it is baking and makes great savoury toast.

Makes 2 loaves

400g strong white flour
100g wholemeal bread flour
1 tsp salt
30g fresh yeast or 10g fast-action dried yeast
400ml warm water
1 tbsp honey
2 tbsp olive oil
leaves from ¼ bunch of sage, chopped
1 tbsp fennel seeds, toasted and crushed

Mix together the flours and salt in a large electric mixer fitted with the dough hook, or in a mixing bowl, and make a well in the centre. If using fresh yeast, break it up and mix with a little of the warm water and the honey (if using dried yeast add it directly to the flours). Add the remaining water and the oil and mix well, then pour into the well in the dry ingredients. Mix together to make a dough. Knead the dough for 5 minutes, in the mixer or by hand on a floured work surface. Put the dough into an oiled bowl, cover and leave somewhere warm until doubled in size.

Tip out the dough on to the floured surface. Add the sage and fennel and knead for 5 minutes to distribute evenly. Divide the dough in half and shape each piece into a long loaf with pointed ends. Set on a greased baking tray. Spray the loaves with water, then cover lightly with clingfilm and leave in a warm place until doubled in size.

Preheat the oven to 200°C/400°F/gas mark 6. Slash the tops of the loaves with diagonal lines. Bake for 20–25 minutes, until light golden and the loaves sound hollow when tapped on the base. Allow to cool on a wire rack before slicing.

·DRIED HEIRLOOM TOMATOES·
ON TOAST

Heirloom tomatoes are old varieties of tomatoes that have been retained for their attributes. When ripe they are full of flavour and colour. This is a delicious brunch dish. The tomatoes can be stored for a week or two in oil in the fridge and used as an ingredient for other dishes too.

Serves 6

6–8 ripe heirloom tomatoes (about 420g in total), each cut into 2cm thick slices
50ml olive oil
1 tsp caster sugar
2 tsp salt
2 cloves garlic, peeled and very thinly sliced
leaves from ¼ bunch of thyme
50ml extra virgin olive oil
6 slices of your favourite artisan bread, for toasting

Preheat the oven to 75°C/150°F/lowest gas mark, and line two baking trays with baking parchment. Arrange the tomato slices on the paper, then drizzle over the olive oil. Sprinkle evenly with the sugar and salt, and place a slice of garlic on each piece. Sprinkle with the thyme leaves. Place in the oven and leave to dry for 6 hours.

Remove the tomatoes from the trays and place in a bowl with the extra virgin olive oil. Cover and leave to macerate for 1 hour. Serve on hot toast with the extra virgin olive oil drizzled on top.

·SPICED FRENCH TOAST·
WITH BURNT HONEY

You may not have tried caramelizing honey before, but it is something
I do recommend. It intensifies the flavour and reduces the sweetness,
making the honey a great addition to any sweet dish.

Serves 4

1 unsliced loaf of your favourite bread
3 free-range eggs
300ml milk
1 tbsp ground cinnamon
1 tsp ground mixed spice
25g caster sugar
½ tsp salt
50g unsalted butter

Burnt honey sauce
100g honey
25g unsalted butter

Cut eight 2cm-thick slices from the loaf. Whisk the eggs with the milk in a wide, shallow dish. Add the slices of bread, one at a time, and thoroughly soak both sides; as they are soaked, pile up on a plate. Mix together the spices, sugar and salt and set aside.

You will probably have to cook the French toast in batches. Heat some of the butter in a frying pan. Dust both sides of each slice of bread with the spice mix, then fry until golden brown on both sides. Remove them from the pan as they are cooked. Fry the remaining slices, adding more butter to the pan as needed. Keep warm.

Wipe out the frying pan, then add the honey. Bring to the boil and caramelize to a deep golden colour. Whisk in the butter, then drizzle the burnt honey over the French toast. Serve immediately.

AFTERNOON TEA

Anna, Duchess of Bedford (1783–1857), one of Queen Victoria's ladies-in-waiting, has been credited with inventing 'afternoon tea'. Anna was quite fond of taking tea with petite-sized cakes in her room during the late afternoon. Many followed the Duchess's lead, and the custom of a small meal or snack eaten late in the day became fashionable.

Towards the end of the 19th century it was firmly entrenched, with Henry James writing: 'There are few hours in life more agreeable than the hour dedicated to the ceremony known as an afternoon tea.' Afternoon tea is a ritual still much enjoyed today, most often in hotels and restaurants.

For me, afternoon tea is all about scones (with lashings of clotted cream and jam), flavoursome sandwiches and a few sweet treats. We serve a great afternoon tea in our bar at The Gilbert Scott, and the bar team have created some wonderful tea-based cocktails for those wishing to partake of a tipple in the afternoon.

· CORONATION CHICKEN · SANDWICHES

Created for the banquet after the coronation of Queen Elizabeth II in 1953, this chicken dish has become the staple filling of many a sandwich since. The version here is less heavy and sweet than most, and makes good canapés to serve with drinks too.

Makes 12 tea sandwiches or 24 small canapés

10g butter
½ onion, peeled and finely sliced
1 tbsp curry powder
50g whole toasted almonds, finely chopped
100g home-made or good-quality purchased mayonnaise
leaves from ¼ bunch of coriander, chopped
2 heaped tbsp whipped cream
1 tbsp dark mango chutney
½ tsp salt
meat from ½ roast chicken, shredded into chunks

To serve
6 slices white or brown bread
soft butter (optional)

Melt the butter in a frying pan. When foaming, add the onion and curry powder and cook until lightly browned. Add the almonds and mix well. Cool, then add to the mayonnaise in a bowl. Add the coriander, cream, chutney and salt, mixing well. Taste and adjust the seasoning, if necessary. Mix in the chicken.

Spread slices of fresh bread lightly with soft butter, if you like. Divide the filling mix among half of the slices, then cover each with another slice of buttered bread. Trim off the crusts, if you wish, then cut into triangles or fingers. Serve immediately.

CANAPÉS
Fill warmed mini pastry cases with the chicken mix. Or make small croûton cases by cutting crustless bread slices into triangles, pressing into greased mini muffin moulds and baking in a preheated 180°C/350°F/gas mark 4 oven for 6–8 minutes, until crisp and golden brown. Garnish the canapés with coriander cress, if you wish.

· RIGHT HONOURABLE · CUCUMBER SANDWICHES

Fit for the finest tea table, these are a bit quirky as the cucumber is on the outside of the sandwich, not the inside. It is important when making cucumber sandwiches that you lightly salt the cucumber for a short period of time, then rinse and dry the slices. This not only seasons the cucumber, it also makes it crunchier. Fresh white bread and a salted English butter are also key to making these sandwiches great.

Makes 12

1 large cucumber, peeled
salt
60g soft, lightly salted butter
12 slices good-quality white bread,
crusts removed

Using a peeler, shave long strips from the cucumber, a third of the length at a time, until you reach the seeds; discard the seeded centre. Lay the strips out on a tray and sprinkle lightly with salt on both sides. Leave for 30 minutes, then rinse well under cold water and pat dry.

Butter both sides of the bread slices. Cover the butter on both sides with the cucumber strips and trim to fit neatly. Set each slice of cucumber-covered bread on a sheet of clingfilm and roll up tightly into a spiral, rolling in the same direction as the way the cucumber slices are lying. Twist the clingfilm at each end of the roll to secure. Chill for 10 minutes.

When ready to serve, trim off the ends, with the clingfilm, then unwrap your inside-out cucumber sandwiches.

·EGG AND CRESS· SANDWICHES

A number of important factors contribute to the perfect egg sandwich. Firstly, the eggs should be cooked so they still retain some wobble in the yolk. Then they need to be combined with good-quality mayonnaise and plenty of seasoning. Ultra-fresh bread, with a good layer of salted butter, is also essential.

Makes 16 tea sandwiches

4 free-range eggs
15g soft unsalted butter
2 tbsp home-made or good-quality purchased mayonnaise
½ tsp salt
freshly ground black pepper to taste
pinch of curry powder
1 punnet of cress, leaves snipped

To serve
8 slices fresh white bread
soft, lightly salted butter

Put the eggs in a small pan of water and bring to the boil, then simmer for 4 minutes. Drain and run under cold water to cool. Peel the eggs and place in a bowl. Mash with a fork, leaving them relatively chunky. Add the butter and mix well. Add the remaining ingredients, except the cress, and stir in. Gently mix in the cress.

Butter the bread. Spread the egg mix on half of the slices and top each with another slice. Cut off the crusts, then cut each sandwich into triangles or fingers and serve as soon as possible.

· YORKSHIRE PARKIN ·

This gingerbread-type cake is great with tea
in the afternoon, or served with blue cheese as
a snack – the salty creaminess of the cheese pairs
perfectly with the sticky, spicy cake. Parkin will
keep for a good 5 days in the fridge.

Cuts into 12 slices

150g unsalted butter
150g dark muscovado sugar
150g treacle
75g golden syrup
150g self-raising flour
150g medium oatmeal
½ tsp salt
15g ground ginger
50ml milk, warmed
2 free-range eggs, beaten

Preheat the oven to 150°C/300°F/gas mark 2.

Combine the butter, sugar, treacle and syrup in
a pan and heat gently until melted and syrupy.
Allow to cool slightly.

Mix all of the dry ingredients in a bowl and
make a well in the centre. Pour in the syrupy
mixture. Add the milk and mix well, then stir
in the beaten eggs. Pour the mix into a greased
and lined 24 x 10cm loaf tin.

Bake for about 1 hour, until a skewer inserted
into the centre comes out clean. Allow to cool in
the tin for 15 minutes, then turn out on to a wire
rack to finish cooling completely.

· SCONES ·

Scone recipes often spark debate. I will say no more than that I think this is one of the best. The trick for success is to avoid overmixing the dough – if you do, the gluten in the flour will develop and the scones will be rubbery and too firm.

Makes 6 large scones

250g self-raising flour
good pinch of salt
25g caster sugar
75g chilled unsalted butter
1 free-range egg, beaten
100ml milk, plus extra for brushing

Preheat the oven to 180°C/350°F/gas mark 4. Combine the flour, salt and sugar in a bowl and rub in the butter until the mix resembles breadcrumbs. Lightly beat together the egg and milk and slowly add to the bowl, stirring just to bring together into a dough, being very careful not to overmix.

Roll out the dough on a floured surface to 5cm thick. Cover and allow to rest for 10 minutes before cutting into 7cm round or square shapes. Transfer to a baking tray and brush with milk, then bake for 20–25 minutes, until golden. Serve warm.

STRAWBERRY AND ROSE JAM

Make this jam at the height of the strawberry season, when the fruit is at its sweetest. Rose water adds a lovely aromatic quality.

Makes 2 medium-size jars

1kg fresh strawberries, halved
50ml lemon juice
250ml rose water
1kg granulated sugar
20g pectin powder

Put the strawberries, lemon juice and rose water in a large saucepan and set over a moderate heat. Mix the sugar and pectin together, then add to the strawberries. Bring the mix to a gentle boil, then cook until the temperature of the jam reaches 104°C. Remove from the heat and ladle into hot sterilized jars, sealing well. Store in a cool, dark place for up to 6 months.

AFTERNOON TEA:

(TOP) SCONES, CLOTTED CREAM AND STRAWBERRY AND ROSE JAM

(MIDDLE) MINI ECCLES CAKES, LEMON DRIZZLE CAKE, MINI ETON MESSS

(BOTTOM) SANDWICHES – EGG AND CRESS, HONOURABLE CUCUMBER AND CORONATION CHICKEN

· WELSH CAKES ·

These are also known as bakestones because in Wales they are traditionally cooked on a bakestone or cast-iron griddle. We serve them at the restaurant with hard cheese and pickle. Their soft texture and sweetness work very well with the saltiness of the cheese. Delicious with butter and jam or honey too.

Makes 12

100g soft unsalted butter, plus extra for frying
75g caster sugar
50g currants
1 free-range egg, lightly beaten
225g plain flour
½ tsp baking powder
pinch of salt

Cream the butter with the sugar until light and fluffy. Add the currants and egg and mix well. Sift the flour, baking powder and salt into the bowl, then fold into the creamed mix. Shape into a log about 5cm in diameter. Wrap in clingfilm and keep in the fridge until required.

When ready to serve, heat a frying pan with a little butter. Cut the log across into 1cm-thick slices. Fry in the hot butter for about 4 minutes on each side, until golden brown and cooked through. Allow to cool before serving.

· MINI ECCLES CAKES ·

Named after the town of Eccles in Greater Manchester, it is not known who created the recipe for these moist, chewy treats, but the first Eccles cakes were sold in a shop in the town centre in 1793. We serve large Eccles cakes in the restaurant as a pudding, with our famous Cheddar cheese ice cream.

Makes 20

Rough puff pastry
250g plain flour
7g salt
250g unsalted butter (remove from the fridge 10 minutes before using)
125ml iced water
milk, for brushing
granulated or caster sugar, for sprinkling

Filling
150g unsalted butter
150g demerara sugar
2 tsp ground cinnamon
2 tsp grated nutmeg
grated zest of 2 oranges
150g golden raisins
150g currants
100g mixed candied peel, chopped

Begin with the pastry. Mix the flour and salt in a bowl. Rub in the butter, leaving it in small lumps, then bind with the water to make a dough. Shape into a neat rectangle, wrap in clingfilm and leave to rest in the fridge for 45 minutes.

Unwrap the pastry rectangle and place it on a floured surface so it is lying vertically in front of you. Fold in a quarter of each short end so they meet in the middle, then fold over in half – this is known as a 'book fold'. Wrap in clingfilm and refrigerate for 45 minutes.

Repeat the rolling out, folding and chilling process two more times. Then roll out the pastry to 5mm thick. Cover and leave to rest on the floured surface for 30 minutes before cutting out 20 discs 8cm in diameter. Arrange on a tray lined with baking parchment and lay another sheet of parchment on top. Place in the fridge to chill for at least 20 minutes.

To make the filling, combine the butter, sugar, spices and zest in a small pan and gently melt. Remove from the heat and add the fruit. Cool, then divide equally into 20 balls.

Take four pastry discs out of the fridge and lay them on a floured surface. Place a ball of filling in the centre of each disc, then fold the pastry around the filling into the centre, to seal in the filling. Flip the cakes over and flatten lightly with your palm. Shape the remaining cakes in the same way.

Preheat the oven to 200°C/400°F/gas mark 6. Arrange the cakes on a baking tray lined with baking paper. Brush them with milk and sprinkle liberally with sugar. Make three small, parallel incisions in the top of each cake. Bake for 12–15 minutes, until golden. Serve warm, or cool on the tray.

·MRS BEETON'S CHEESE· BUTTERFLIES

Another great recipe idea from Mrs Beeton, these 'butterflies' consist of a short, savoury biscuit with a cheese mousse piped on top and two small semi-circles of biscuit pushed in to look like wings. We use a goat's cheese mousse but you can substitute another soft or blue cheese if you prefer.

Makes 12

Biscuits
100g plain flour
pinch of English mustard powder
pinch of cayenne pepper
pinch of salt
75g butter
75g Parmesan cheese, grated
1 free-range egg yolk
25–50ml cold water

Cheese mousse
25g cream cheese
50g soft goat's cheese
pinch of salt

Preheat the oven to 180°C/350°F/gas mark 4. Sift the flour, mustard, cayenne and salt together. Cream the butter until pale and fluffy, then add the flour mix with the Parmesan, mixing well. Add the egg yolk and enough cold water to bring together to make a stiff dough. Roll out on a floured surface to 5mm thick. Lift on to a tray and chill for 25 minutes.

Remove the sheet of dough from the fridge and cut out 24 discs using a 3cm round cutter. Cut half of the discs in half to form the butterfly wings. Place the discs and 'wings' on a greased baking tray and bake for 8–10 minutes, until lightly golden. Cool on the tray.

For the mousse, put the cream cheese in a bowl and beat until smooth. Put the goat's cheese in another bowl and break down with a spatula, mixing until smooth. Combine the two cheeses and season with salt to taste. Spoon into a piping bag fitted with a plain 5mm nozzle. Set aside.

When the biscuits have cooled, pipe the cheese mousse on to the round biscuits. Add a pair of 'wings' to each, pushing pointed ends into the mousse with the flat sides almost touching, so the 'wings' stand out. Serve as soon as possible.

BAKEWELL TART

The earliest incarnation of this tart, Bakewell pudding,
is said to have originated in the 1860s in the market town of
Bakewell in Derbyshire. Our version of the tart is a slightly
different take on the classic, with a cherry jelly instead of jam.

Makes 12 slices

Sweet pastry
85g soft unsalted butter
115g caster sugar
225g strong flour
7g baking powder
3g salt
100ml double cream

Almond layer
250g unsalted butter
250g ground almonds
375g caster sugar
45g plain flour
340g (about 11) free-range egg whites

Cherry jelly
1 x 340g jar cherry jam
250ml cherry juice
juice of 1 lemon
6 leaves gelatine

Almond icing
200g icing sugar
2 tbsp hot water
a few drops of almond essence
glacé cherries, to finish

For the sweet pastry, mix the soft butter and sugar together
with an electric mixer on slow speed, or in a food processor,
until just combined. Sift the flour, baking powder and salt
together. Add half to the butter and mix to form a smooth
paste, then add the remaining flour and mix just until fine
crumbs are formed. Slowly add the cream, mixing only to
bind to a dough. Gather into a ball, wrap in clingfilm and
place in the fridge to rest for 1 hour.

Grease a baking tray approximately 20 x 28cm and line with
baking parchment. Roll out the pastry dough between two
sheets of baking parchment until 5mm thick. Allow to rest
in the fridge for 20 minutes, then cut into a rectangle to fit
the prepared baking tray. Line the tray with the pastry, then
place in the fridge to chill while you make the almond mix.

Heat the butter in a saucepan until it melts and foams, then
whisk until it turns dark brown. Remove from the heat and
set aside to cool. Stir together the ground almonds, sugar and
flour in a bowl, then mix in the egg whites followed by the
browned butter (beurre noisette) until homogenous. Set aside.

Preheat the oven to 180°C/350°F/gas mark 4. Place the
baking tray in the oven and bake the pastry for 12 minutes,
until set and golden brown. Spread the almond mix evenly
over the pastry. Return to the oven and bake for 20 minutes,
until the almond layer is golden and cooked through. Remove
from the oven and leave to cool.

For the jelly, put the jam and the juices into a saucepan, bring to a simmer and cook for 10 minutes, skimming off any foam that forms. Meanwhile, soak the gelatine leaves in a little cold water for 5 minutes to soften. Squeeze out the water, then add the gelatine to the cherry mix and stir until melted. Line a baking tray the same size as that used for the almond base (approximately 20 x 28cm) with a double layer of clingfilm. Pour the cherry mixture into the lined tray and refrigerate until set.

Turn out the set jelly on to a board and slice 5mm off the two shorter ends. Put the slices into a saucepan to melt. Brush the top of the almond layer with the melted jelly, then place the sheet of set jelly on top.

To make the icing, sift the icing sugar into a bowl, add the hot water and essence, and stir until smooth. Spread the icing evenly over the sheet of jelly. Chill to set before cutting into slices and garnishing with glacé cherries.

· CARROT CAKE ·

Carrots have been used in sweet cakes since medieval times. Then, sweeteners such as sugar were scarce and expensive whereas carrots, which contain more sugar than any other vegetable, were much easier to come by. Today we use carrots less in sweet baking, with the exception of this always popular moist and flavoursome cake.

Makes 1 large cake or 12 muffin-size cakes

3 free-range eggs
150g caster sugar
180g peeled grated carrots
100g tinned crushed pineapple
50g walnuts, chopped
1 tsp grated orange zest
100ml groundnut oil
150g self-raising flour
½ tsp bicarbonate of soda
pinch of salt
1 tsp ground cinnamon

Icing
100g soft unsalted butter
200g icing sugar, sifted
200g cream cheese
grated zest and juice of 1 lemon

Preheat the oven to 180°C/350°F/gas mark 4. Combine the eggs, sugar, carrots, pineapple, walnuts, orange zest and oil in a mixing bowl. Sift the flour, bicarbonate of soda, salt and cinnamon into another bowl. Gently fold into the egg mixture. Divide equally among 12 greased muffin tins or a 25cm cake tin. Bake for about 20 minutes (or about 25 minutes for a large cake), until a skewer inserted into the centre of a cake comes out clean. Cool in the tins for 10–15 minutes, then finish cooling on a wire rack.

To make the icing, cream the butter with the sugar until white and fluffy. Beat the cream cheese until soft, then add to the butter mix with the lemon zest and juice, mixing well. For small cakes, put the icing into a piping bag fitted with a 1cm nozzle and pipe a large dollop on top of each one. For a large cake, swirl the icing over the top using a palette knife.

·117·
·CHEDDAR CHEESE STRAWS·

Cheddar cheese originated in the village of Cheddar in Somerset where caves in the Gorge, on the edge of the village, provide the ideal humidity and temperature for the maturing of the cheese. Records show that Cheddar cheese has been produced since the 12th century.

Makes 12

250g plain flour
175g strong Cheddar cheese (Cornish Cruncher is a favourite)
pinch of salt
freshly ground black pepper to taste
½ tsp smoked paprika
125g cold unsalted butter, cubed
2 free-range egg yolks
25–50ml cold water

Preheat the oven to 180°C/350°F/gas mark 4. Mix together the flour, cheese, salt, four turns of the peppermill and the paprika in a large bowl. Using your fingertips, rub the butter into the mix until it resembles breadcrumbs. Add the egg yolks and enough cold water to bring the crumbs together into a dough.

Turn out the dough on to a well-floured surface and carefully roll out to a rectangle 5mm thick. Trim the edges straight, then cut the pastry into strips 2cm wide and place on a greased baking tray. Gently twist each strip to create a curled effect, then bake for 15–20 minutes, until golden. Cool on a wire rack, then store in an airtight container.

· TEA CAKES ·

I love chocolate tea cakes. Smothered in milk chocolate (or dark if you prefer), they are a great afternoon treat with a large mug of builder's tea.

Makes 6

Marshmallow
4 leaves gelatine
500g caster sugar
250ml water

Biscuits
75g soft unsalted butter
50g icing sugar, sifted
1 free-range egg yolk
100g plain flour

6 tsp raspberry jam
150g dark or milk chocolate, chopped

Lightly oil six 8cm half-sphere moulds. For the marshmallow, soak the gelatine in cold water for 10 minutes. Meanwhile, put the sugar and water in a saucepan and set over a moderate heat. When the sugar has dissolved, bring to the boil and boil for 10 minutes. Remove from the heat. Squeeze excess water from the gelatine, add to the sugar syrup and stir until melted. Pour into a mixing bowl and beat with an electric mixer until the mixture is light and fluffy and has cooled.

Using a spatula, smooth spoonfuls of the marshmallow into the moulds. Smooth over the tops of the moulds with a palette knife so the marshmallows will have a flat base. Place in the fridge to set for 1 hour. When ready to use, gently pop them out of their moulds by pushing the mould inwards.

For the biscuits, cream the butter with the sugar until soft and fluffy. Add the egg yolk and flour and mix until just combined. Shape the biscuit dough into a ball, wrap in clingfilm and chill for 25 minutes.

Unwrap the biscuit dough and roll out between two sheets of baking parchment to 5mm thickness. Put back in the fridge to rest for 25 minutes while preheating your oven to 175°C/350°F/gas mark 4. Then cut into six 8.5cm rounds and place on a greased baking tray. Bake for 8–10 minutes, until lightly golden. Allow to cool.

Smooth 1 teaspoon of jam over each biscuit, then set a marshmallow dome on top.

Melt the chocolate in a small heatproof bowl set over a pan of simmering water. Using a pastry brush, liberally brush the bottom of each biscuit with chocolate, then set on a tray lined with baking parchment. Liberally cover the marshmallow dome and the sides of the biscuit with more chocolate, using the pastry brush to smooth it over. Place in the fridge to set.

SUPER-CHOCOLATEY BROWNIE

Chocolate is a required element in any afternoon tea selection, and these brownies fit the bill perfectly. Because the chocolate flavour is so important, be sure to use the best dark chocolate, with at least 70 per cent cocoa solids.

Cuts into 12 slices

225g unsalted butter
100g dark chocolate (minimum 70% cocoa solids), broken up
4 free-range eggs
200g caster sugar
50g plain flour
50g cocoa powder
75g walnuts, chopped
75g dark chocolate (minimum 70% cocoa solids), chopped

Preheat the oven to 160°C/325°F/gas mark 3. Put the butter and broken up chocolate in a heavy-based pan and melt gently. When smooth, remove from the heat. Whisk the eggs and sugar together in a bowl, then add to the chocolate mix and stir. Sift the flour and cocoa together, then fold into the chocolate mix. Stir in the walnuts and chopped chocolate.

Grease a baking dish or tin about 22 x 14cm and 3cm deep, then line with baking parchment. Pour in the brownie mix. Bake for 25 minutes, until a skewer inserted into the centre comes out clean. Cool in the dish, then cut into slices.

·LEMON DRIZZLE CAKE·

An old-fashioned tea cake, this is simple to make yet delicious. We serve it in small slices as part of our afternoon tea offering, with a rich lemon curd piped on top.

Serves 8–10

200g unsalted butter
300g caster sugar, plus extra for sprinkling
3 free-range eggs, beaten
grated zest and juice of 3 lemons
250g self-raising flour
½ tsp bicarbonate of soda
100ml milk
good-quality purchased lemon curd,
for serving

Preheat the oven to 180°C/350°F/gas mark 4. Cream the butter with 250g of the sugar until light and fluffy. Add the eggs and lemon zest and mix well. Sift the flour and bicarbonate of soda into the bowl and gently mix in. Add the milk and bring together until just combined.

Pour the mix into a greased and lined 24 x 10cm loaf tin. Bake for about 25 minutes, until a skewer inserted into the centre of the cake comes out clean.

Heat the lemon juice with the remaining 50g sugar to create a syrup.

While the cake is still warm, prick it all over the top with a skewer, then evenly drizzle the lemon syrup over the surface. Finish with a sprinkle of caster sugar. Leave to cool in the tin.

Serve each slice with a good dollop of lemon curd.

· FIG ROLLS ·

Home-made fig rolls are far superior to the packet
you reach for in the supermarket. Give this recipe
a try and you will see what I mean.

Makes about 12

300g soft dried figs, diced
50ml crème de figue (fig liqueur) or brandy

Pastry
85g soft unsalted butter
115g caster sugar, plus extra for sprinkling
225g plain flour
5g baking powder
pinch of salt
100ml double cream
milk, for brushing

Put the diced figs into a saucepan with the alcohol
and heat until they become soft. Purée half of them
in a blender; mix this with the remaining diced figs.
Allow to cool, then divide the mix into four and roll
up each portion in clingfilm to create a sausage shape
about 2cm in diameter and 20cm long. Place these
'sausages' in the freezer to firm up.

Cream the butter with the sugar until light and fluffy.
Sift the flour, baking powder and salt into the bowl and
mix in, then slowly add the cream, mixing until just
combined. Shape into a ball, cover with clingfilm and
refrigerate for 25 minutes.

Remove the pastry from the fridge and divide in half.
Roll out each portion between two sheets of baking
parchment to a rectangle 5mm thick and about 20 x 10cm.
Trim the edges, then cut each rectangle lengthways in half.
Unwrap one of the fig 'sausages' and place on one long
edge of a pastry strip. Brush the other long edge of the
pastry strip with milk, then roll the pastry over the fig
to enclose, pressing well to seal. Repeat the process with
the other fig 'sausages' and pastry strips. Wrap the finished
logs in clingfilm and place in the fridge to firm up.

Preheat the oven to 180°C/350°F/gas mark 4. Remove
the logs from the fridge and unwrap. Brush with milk, then
sprinkle with caster sugar. Trim off the ends of each log,
then cut across into four pieces. Place on a greased baking
tray, seam side down. Bake for 15–20 minutes, until
golden. Leave to cool on the tray for 10–15 minutes, then
serve warm. Or transfer to a wire rack to cool completely.

INDEX

·OUR FAVOURITE SUPPLIERS·

BEEF:
Lake District Farmers http://www.lakedistrictfarmers.co.uk

PORK:
Great Garnetts Farm http://www.greatgarnetts.co.uk

GAME:
Yorkshire Game http://www.yorkshiregame.co.uk

FISH:
Fish for Thought http://www.martins-seafresh.co.uk

SMOKED SALMON:
Brown & Forrest http://www.smokedeel.co.uk

OYSTERS:
Wright Brothers http://thewrightbrothers.co.uk

SNAILS:
Dorset Escargot http://www.dorsetsnails.co.uk

OLIVES AND OLIVE OIL:
Fresh Olive Company http://www.fresholive.com

BUTTER:
Netherend Farm http://www.netherendfarmbutter.co.uk

CHEESE:
La Fromagerie http://www.lafromagerie.co.uk

BREAD:
The Flour Station http://www.theflourstation.com

VEGETABLES:
Natoora http://www.natoora.co.uk

HONEY:
London Honey Man http://www.thelondonhoneycompany.co.uk

ENGLISH SPARKLING WINE:
Nyetimber http://www.nyetimber.com

COOK'S NOTES

Eggs used in the recipes are size medium, unless otherwise specified.

Herbs are measured in bunches or fractions of a bunch; a bunch weighs about 15g.

Lemon zest is best grated, or taken with a zester, from unwaxed lemons.

Oven temperatures given in recipes are for fan ovens.

Salt and pepper are not in ingredients lists, unless specific quantities are given. I've assumed that all cooks will season with salt and pepper to taste.

· ACKNOWLEDGEMENTS ·

Thanks must be given firstly to Harry Handelsman for being a visionary risk taker!

A big thank you to Kevin Kelly and the team at the St Pancras Hotel for being wonderful partners in a great venture.

To Sergio Coimbra (photographer), who is one of the kindest, most generous and talented people I have had the pleasure of meeting. Thanks also to Luciana Bianchi for helping me in her native home of Brazil and introducing us to Sergio.

To Matt Hall and the White Label team for their passion and creativity (and strange cat stories).

To the Transworld team for giving us the opportunity to showcase our wondrous restaurant and bar.

To my treasured family: Jane, my wife, and my three children, Jake, Archie and Jessie.

To the team at my restaurant at the Berkeley Hotel for their continued support and dedication.

To the opening team alumni: Oliver Blackburn (Bar Manager), Dominique Corrolleur (Floor Manager), Samantha Dinsdale (Pastry Chef), Claire O'Dowd (Reception and Reservations Manager), Oliver Wilson (Head Chef).

To the current team: Mark Cesareo (Restaurant Manager), Dav Eames (Bar Manager), Nick Ward (Head Chef).

Anastasija Popova, Giancarlo Cuccuru, Sangram Shinde, Rasa Potiomkina, Duncan Edgeley. Dorota Goksal, Francisco (Frankie) Benitez Coboz, Conrad Pohlinger, Shauna Caithness, Sarah Holah. Rhys Evans, Giulia Carboni. Davide Nizzola, Ama Fru, Laura Castellano, Toheed Arshad, Riccardo Trevisan, Stanislav Andrusjevic. François Marsal, Pawel Olszowski, Cristina Szakal, Mariann Rinfel, Donatas Sickus, Adam Kiss, Ildelfonso Fernadez, William Sanchos, Daniel Esteva, Enrique Baresquin, Federico Bassani, Ali Mehrfar, Richard Gomes de Sena, Mithun Cox. Adam Wood, Thomas Sargent, Dahiyah Yunos, Dale Deakin, Rhys Roberts, Nicholas Cantos, Pradeep Kosireddy, Tamas Patko, Tibor Rekasi, Marlon Clarke.

OPPOSITE:
(LEFT TO RIGHT):
CHANTELLE NICHOLSON (GENERAL MANAGER),
SERGIO COIMBRA (PHOTOGRAPHER), MARCUS WAREING

THANK YOU